THE TRUMPET SHALL SOUND

BY MAURICE BARBANELL

Foreword by

HANNEN SWAFFER

"In a moment, in the twinkling of an eye, at the last trump; for the trumpet shall sound, and the dead shall be raised incorruptible. . ."

I CORINTHIANS 15:52

The Spiritual Truth Press

First Impression 1933
This Edition October 2020

ISBN 978-1-9998571-4-1

www.spiritualtruthfoundation.org

CONTENTS

A BRIEF INTRODUCTION TO THIS NEW EDITION

The Trumpet Shall Sound is one of more than a dozen books and pamphlets written by Maurice Barbanell, founding editor of the Spiritualist newspaper *Psychic News*. It was first published in 1933. As I write, it has been out of print for decades but is such an exceptionally fine record of evidential spirit communication that rare copies from second-hand booksellers around the world have sold for three-figure sums.

The book consists entirely of verbatim conversations between spirit individuals and their earthly loved ones, which took place through the Direct Voice mediumship of the legendary Estelle Roberts between 1932 and 1933.

These sittings were held in a small room in Estelle Roberts' home under the direct control of her guide, Red Cloud, who had complete authority over which visitors would be invited to attend the circle – always on the basis of the greatest need.

Maurice Barbanell was one of Estelle's four regular home circle members and was present for almost all the two-world conversations which unfolded. Those conversations, providing detailed evidence that the spirit communicators were fully aware of the minutiae of their earthly loved ones' day-today lives, were faithfully noted down by a stenographer seated in a curtained-off corner of the room.

The evidence of survival beyond death obtained in these sittings is some of the most compelling ever recorded. It includes the famous case of Bessy Manning, a young spirit girl who came to make a simple and heartfelt request – that someone would contact her grieving mother.

No one present had known Bessie, and no one knew her mother. But this was no barrier for Bessie, who simply asked Maurice Barbanell to write to her mother – and provided him with the address! You can read their extraordinary story and life-changing two-world conversation in Chapters 21 and 22.

It has been a special privilege to play a role in bringing this unique book back into print on behalf of the Spiritual Truth Foundation. Many years ago, after a crippling bereavement, I myself was one of those lucky people who just happened to find a copy on a second-hand book website when I needed it most.

Susan Farrow
Publications Director
The Spiritual Truth Foundation
September 2020

THE UPPER ROOM
A FOREWORD
BY HANNEN SWAFFER

"THESE are the dead ones," said Red Cloud one night, interposing his friendly, dominating, challenging personality as a short interval between two séance-room dramas.

I have been present at nearly three hundred of them during the last few months.

Maurice Barbanell tells of them in The Trumpet Shall Sound in detail, analysing the evidence with which they were crowded, describing them at length.

I merely sum them up.

I am used to tense incident in the world of the theatre, yes, and in the greater drama of wider life outside. Yet many of the happenings so well described in the pages that follow are among the most remarkable experiences of my crowded life.

It was the direct voice which convinced me of Spiritualism—Dennis Bradley's own mediumship, suddenly developed in his own home.

I sat, afterwards, at over a score of direct-voice séances at which George Valiantine was the medium. At one of them held in the light, when Valiantine and I were the only people present, I heard a spirit voice speaking from a trumpet held nearly a yard from the medium's mouth.

I have sat with Mrs. Roberts Johnson, and Evan Powell, and other direct-voice mediums. But, to my mind, the Estelle Roberts phenomena are by far the best evidence of their kind of which modern Spiritualism can produce a record.

Once a fortnight, all specially invited by Red Cloud him-self, we have gathered at Teddington, gone upstairs into a room used only for these séances, and there sat for two hours or so, about a score of us. Nearly all the sitters have invariably been strangers. And yet, for two hours on end, evidence has poured from the Other World.

Sometimes the medium has known some of the sitters' names. Sometimes she has sat with them before for trance, or met them in the world outside. But often they have been complete strangers to her.

The evidence is unchallengeable.

On every occasion but one, every new sitter, or crowd of sitters, for sometimes two, or even three, come together, has heard the voice of a "dead" friend, bringing messages of con-solation, uttering words of comfort, adding to the continued chorus which pours from the Other Side.

"We are not dead," they say.

I have known it change people's lives. I have seen hope brighten their eyes again.

If it could happen in every town, it would change the world. There is no payment. You are warned not to volunteer evidence. You are asked, before each sitting, not to suggest a name, or give one fact.

"Your spirit friends will prove themselves." That is always the warning before it starts. "Say nothing." It started two years ago, merely because Mrs. Roberts wished to help another medium, who was in straitened circumstances. She thought that, if she could develop the direct voice, she could charge for her sittings and raise some money. For eighteen months, under Mrs. Constance Treloar's direction, she and a small group sat. Then, one night, the Voice came.

For a time the sittings were held with the object for which they began. Then, one night, Red Cloud said, "The medium needs no more help. In future I will invite the sitters."

So, once a fortnight, it still goes on—merely so that mourners shall be comforted.

Yes, in that upper room at Teddington, I have heard the voices of people who were thought to have been suicides prove that it was not suicide, but an accident.

I have known spirit friends return to distressed parents, or children, with proof that death, after all, was only a short step further on.

I have heard tears of joy wept often in that upper room, so great was the consolation. Yes, and under the stress, I have often wept myself.

Mind you, it is all in the dark, thick, impenetrable darkness, for Red Cloud objects if there is the slightest pin-prick of light.

And yet, although you can see nothing except the phosphorescence on the trumpet's mouth, you can often visualise the spirit people who are talking from the other end. They have character and personality, and they differ, every one of them, from all the others.

At first, sometimes, a new spirit talks in a whisper. Then, gradually, his voice gathers strength. If he returns at some later sitting, it takes on a tone, and is not merely a voice, but a living man or woman.

Some of the voices become so characteristic that, the moment you hear them, you know from past experience whose they are.

"Oh! Is it you, Jackie?" you hear from the sitters who have

been before, as they recognise the voice of one child who often returns to his foster-parent. Then there is Louise, who was a girl dancer—one who said, one night, "They did not tell me that I was a little German girl. They did not want to hurt me."

"We can't see you," I said to one spirit voice, heard regularly. A laugh came.

"Why, you must be dead," was the amused answer.

There is another spirit voice I always know, that of a young woman who was a Girl Guide, and who always insists that she has two names, Helen Isabel, and corrects anything you wrongly remember about her.

Sceptics insist that we stupid Spiritualists say, "Is that you, Granny?"

At the Estelle Roberts sitting, all that sort of thing is a joke. So often has Mrs. Treloar said, in warning, "Do not say 'Is that you, Tom? or Dick, or Harry,'" that sometimes Red Cloud mockingly says, when an unusual name has been given:

"That was not Dick."

Sometimes we have said, "That was a good bit of telepathy, Red Cloud," or asked, "Can you give us some more subconscious mind?

"It is in the medium's book," he has replied more than once, this being a joke about the conjurers, who say that mediums circulate a book in which are recorded the names and addresses of all the friends and relatives of people who are expected to make a round of Spiritualist societies.

Almost every variety of human experience is part of these sittings—love scenes, family reunions, meetings of old friends. Quarrels have been made up. Pacts have been kept.

"I have got a good one coming now," Red Cloud has said before a dramatic bit of evidence, adding what he always says before another voice comes through, "Hold on!"

Then there has started another five-minute drama, a story, acted in the dark, of how someone died and found he was not dead, and then came back with his message of love and proof.

All the time, in an alcove carefully partitioned off and lit inside so that not a particle of brightness can disturb the sitting, a stenographer has sat, taking down every word of the evidence.

Sometimes, when Red Cloud has known it was important, he has shouted, before, "Take this one down, Ivy." Then there has poured through a string of names, fact after fact. . .

Red Cloud cannot be described. When you know him you love him, so full is he of wisdom, kindness and helpfulness.

He never speaks ill of anybody and never condemns. Often he breaks into poetry, blank verse and rhyme mixed up, much of it perfect metre and rhythm and occasionally almost Shakespearean in its beauty.

He typifies all that we understand by the highest conception of love. He will not accept thanks. His inevitable reply to "Thank you, Red Cloud" is, "Don't thank me. Thank God."

Sometimes he will add, "I am only the servant." His sense of humour is acute, bantering at times. He is like lightning at repartee.

Often he uses language so beautiful that you find tears in your eyes, and you are glad it is dark. Sometimes he quotes modern poetry which the medium has never read. When asked where he obtains it, he tells you he has access to all the literature and poetry that has ever been written.

He speaks of the "Council" on the Other Side. He

personifies a Plan.

His knowledge of the Bible is amazing. Yet although he prefers to be known as an Indian, I feel certain it is only a cloak that hides his real self.

"Judge me by my works," he insists, when you ask. Red Cloud never forgets. He will remind you of many things long after you have forgotten them.

"I told you that," he says often. Then you remember.

The case of Sir Henry Segrave most closely concerns me. Segrave, before his passing, used to come to my flat, enquiring into the phenomena of Spiritualism. On the Sunday after his passing, he made his first return. I wrote the next day to his wife:

"MY DEAR LADY SEGRAVE,

"I will not worry you, at this moment, with what would seem to be conventional words about your terrible loss. After all, your dear husband's death is deplored by everybody in the country, and it would be idle. of me to try and express what is, in a sense, a national loss.

"Everywhere I go I hear nothing but kind things about poor de Hane. He was almost the most popular man in England, and we all remember of him, not only his great courage, but his charm and kindliness.

"You must try and remember that he died for his country quite as much as a man dies in battle—and at a time, too, when the nation needs such deeds as his to remind us of what our best people are capable.

"I do not know whether I ought to tell you, because I always tread on such ground very delicately, but Mrs. Swaffer and I had a remarkable experience last night which I feel you should be told about. If you are upset, you must pardon my good intentions.

"We had been talking a lot about de Hane all day, especially as Jimmy Day had mentioned in that morning's Sunday Express one of his visits to our flat, and then when we went into the Plaza Theatre we were shocked to see, on the screen, a picture of his last race.

"Then, returning home, we were alone, because the servant was away. We had left in the drawing-room the Sunday Express, open at the page in which de Hane's last article appeared. As the servant was away, I said, ' Let us have supper in the kitchen.'

"I had been into the bedroom and left on the light over the bed, the one which your husband was very interested in himself when we explained to him materialisations which had taken place immediately under it.

"After supper, I went back in the bedroom, and forgetting I had left the light on, found it dark and turned on the switch. No light came. Then Mrs. Swaffer went into the room a little later, called me, after having turned on the other light, and pointed to the electric light bulb which was in the fire-place. "No earthly hands could have put it there, for it was the one which I had left lighted a few minutes before. If it had fallen, it would have fallen on the bed. It could not have got into the fire-place, for it would have had to climb over a tiled fender. Had it fallen where it was found, it would have crashed into a thousand pieces, for it was on a hard surface. Yet, when the bulb was put back in the lamp, it lit immediately, for not even the filament was broken.

"Then we noticed that the Sunday Express which we had left in the drawing-room was on the bed. We took it back into the drawing-room and discussed the matter, and then, when we returned to the bedroom, found that again the Sunday Express was on the bed.

"I cannot, of course, draw any scientific deduction from what happened last night, but I do believe that it was de Hane, making a first effort to get through. Whoever it was had chosen, for his proof of supernormal power, the most delicate object in the room, and had then twice moved a paper on which the only open page was full of two articles about Sir Henry Segrave.

"I do feel that a cool reasoning brain like his would, after coming to me, perhaps the only link he knew of, choose some such very difficult thing to do.

"Anyway, whether this was Sir Henry Segrave or not, do take it from me, as somebody who has had proof, that, in the hour of your trouble, your dear husband is very near you, and that his loss is only a physical one.

"In another world he is finding work to do, work for which his great qualities have prepared him, work more important than any he could find here, some of which, I am sure, will consist in guarding and protecting your dear self to which he was devotedly attached."

I received the following reply

"DEAR MR. SWAFFER,

"I want to thank you for your kind and gentle letter of sympathy. I much appreciated all you told me, and was not at all upset. His spirit is with me, and is supporting me more than I thought it possible, and it is only at moments that I realise my utter desolation."

Then, over a year later, I received from Lady Segrave the following:

"DEAR MR. SWAFFER,

"I've wondered so often in the past sixteen months whether you have had any communication with my de Hane? I have myself had some very interesting experiences, but nothing very definite so far, and as I've just finished reading your book, which interested me enormously, I venture to write to you, and would be so grateful if you'd tell me anything you know.

"Having descended to the depths of hell I have now found the ' peace of God which passeth all understanding,' and although my life here seems meaningless and futile, I have something glorious to look forward to. Forgive me if I bore you, but in the kindness of your heart, I feel you'll understand."

So began Lady Segrave's enquiry. She came, one night, to my home circle, where my own trance medium, a highly-cultured singer, was being developed. On the first occasion, her husband tried to speak to her, but both he and Lady Segrave were too full of emotion.

Then she went, unknown except to Barbanell, to the Red Cloud direct-voice circle—and heard her husband's voice.

Since then, every fortnight, Segrave has returned to that séance-room to hold converse with his wife.

When I first saw her after the tragedy of her husband's last act of bravery, she was a broken woman.

Now she lives for these fortnightly talks with him. Gradually, she has bloomed out again into the happiness of the womanhood which she enjoyed when first I knew her during his earth life.

Segrave always comes through last, at the Red Cloud sittings. He is by far the most intelligent of all the communicators.

His pleasant, easy charm of manner has adapted itself perfectly, it would seem, with the methods of communication. His perfect politeness, which marked him on earth, is a thing distinctive in itself in the séance-room.

Whenever someone whom he knew on earth has been present, or there has been sitting a medium through whom he has been able to manifest, he has always made himself known as though he were at some reception.

For a moment, it is almost as formal as a drawing-room. Then he starts continuing again the conversation of a fortnight since.

The Segrave case alone would prove Survival beyond doubt.

Far too many churches, faced with the problem of how to comfort the mourners, have recited texts that no longer have much meaning, and read little bits from a book that concerns happenings hundreds of miles away, two thousand years ago.

This book deals with similar happenings in London today.

Not one of the witnesses of the Bible records can be called. Not one of the original documents from which the Old and New Testaments were translated can be traced. Not one word of it can be supported by a fact, or explained otherwise than by a theory.

"You must have faith," say the Churches when you ask.

But in the case of the incidents described by Maurice Barbanell in this book, all the witnesses, so far as I know, are still alive. Their names and addresses are known. Their evidence is at the disposal of anyone who cares to challenge it. And their stories have gone all over the world.

Lady Segrave has told hers, so that all can read. Lady Caillard, whose husband, Sir Vincent, I remember in earth life, has also told her story.

The Earl of Cottenham, an old friend of Segrave's—I knew him long before all this began—is a third who has come forward valiantly with the great Truth, new to many, but, although the Churches suppress it, really as old as the earth.

Scores of lesser-known people have told their story to friends. Some of them hide it, and get no more to tell. Some of them proudly proclaim it and get more evidence.

So it is going on all over the world. Nothing can stop it. Death is its great propagandist. Bereavement is the grief that advertises its real need.

As more and more people die, and as more and more Churches become more stupid and ignorant, so must this great Knowledge grow. And for every spirit that has come back at Red Cloud's circle, a thousand are waiting to return.

"Armistice Day took to the spirit world not vibrations of peace, but vibrations of war," said a spirit to me recently.

"Drums, bugles, rifles and the firing of maroons—that's all war, not peace.

"Why do they all make speeches?

"There are still a lot of soldier boys who have never been back—who cannot get back because there are so few mediums—whose friends would not listen if they came.

"They give up hope.

"Their friends put flowers on their graves. They put on black. They cry.

"Then, when the boys come back, the Church says, 'It's evil spirits.'

"We pull people in to do work, and when they do not do it, we cast them aside. The phenomena, the spirit pictures, the mediumship, the healing, they are not enough. They are largely the toys. Do not mistake the toys for the great thing.

"Talking with Tom, Dick and Harry is not the great work. It is important that people who have lost their loved ones should be helped. But the great work is that you should strive for peace, find homes for the people, see that there is food for all.

"Tell them that there is a bigger war than beating the Germans. It is a war against all the evil in the world, all the tyranny, all the pride."

Then Conan Doyle, speaking through the same Medium, said, "We can only touch one soul here and there. Pull together. There is so much darkness, and we can bring only a little light. But we are winning. In spite of the Church, we shall win."

The crowd of those who listen is large. The host of those who want to listen is legion.

If we could accommodate all those who yearn to attend Red Cloud's direct voice séance, it would fill the Albert Hall.

Letters pour in, every day, to Mrs. Roberts, to Maurice Barbanell, to myself, and to all those who know Mrs. Roberts begging for an invitation.

The answer is, of course, that while the priests slate us, and the Churches condemn, and Pomp and Vanity, and Prejudice and Pride stand arrayed, in their might, against us, death will always remain the most tragic thing of human experience. We know that it is only an incident.

Yet what Mrs. Roberts did—and this is the great lesson of this book—perhaps you can do.

Psychic power is not peculiar to Spiritualism. Mediumship is the private possession of no person, or class, or creed, or colour, or race, or age. It is the most universal thing in the world, except the love which it would spread, and the clamour for human happiness which screams in all the desolate places of the earth.

"Lo, I am with you always, even unto the end of the world," said a great Leader, once.

That is true, also, of our "dead" who have passed on.

Do the Churches not care?

Mourners do. . . And, slowly, we are teaching them.

THE SÉANCE

THE séances are always held in the house of the medium, Mrs. Estelle Roberts, in an upper room not used for any other purpose. It is only a small room and will hold about twenty-five people seated in a circle. The circle is composed of four or five regular sitters, the rest are there at the invitation of Red Cloud or with his approval.

Mrs. Constance Treloar is in charge all the time. Much of the success of the séances is due to her charming personality. She encourages the spirit voices, which are generally weak at first, gives wise counsel to new-comers and leads the singing when it is necessary.

The séances are always held in darkness. Often at the beginning Red Cloud complains that he can see a chink of light. He says it interferes with the psychic rods he has to make.

Two trumpets are used, ordinary tin trumpets with a strip of phosphorescence painted round the broad end. You can always see when the trumpets move. The extraordinary thing is, that no matter how quickly they move, they never make a mistake in the dark. They never fumble, they never bump against anybody, nor touch the wrong person. It is obvious that the intelligences who use them can see perfectly.

The shorthand-writer who records the sittings is seated in a small alcove which has been partitioned off. This enables her to have a red light and to hear all the voices which come through.

The rest of the sitters just take their seats. They are told to link their hands with their neighbours. Then Mrs. Roberts gives an invocation. Soon you hear rather stertorous breathing, an indication that she is being entranced.

Her séances always start with "Onward, Christian Soldiers," then an electric gramophone is played. It plays all the time during the sitting. After a while you do not notice the music. Singing and music give vibrations which are helpful to the spirit voices. Strangely enough the record always played is "Rose Marie," the Drury Lane musical comedy.

After the circle has been started for about ten minutes you see one of the trumpets move. This always gives me a thrill. Soon the voice of Red Cloud is heard, "God bless you all."

THE BOY SUICIDE

IN conversation with Estelle Roberts, one day, she told me about her voice mediumship. I looked at her in surprise. I knew of her as a remarkable trance medium and the foremost public clairvoyant in England.

"Would you like to come to a voice sitting?" she asked.

"Yes, I would."

"I will ask Red Cloud, my guide."

Several days later, she informed me that Red Cloud had invited me to be present at a voice séance.

At the earlier sittings I did not have a shorthand-writer present, and the conversations which I narrate in this chapter have been set down from memory.

Mrs. Madge Donohoe, a friend of mine, asked Red Cloud for permission to bring a friend. Two weeks later she brought a gentleman with her. He was not introduced by name to Mrs. Roberts or to any of the sitters. Later, I learned that he was not a Spiritualist and this was his first séance.

After one of the spirit voices had given some fine evidence, Red Cloud said, "Two thousand years of Christianity and they still say fraud, evil spirits and Beelzebub. Hold on!"

He always says "Hold on!" before each spirit voice speaks. "This is for the new little man." To Red Cloud we are all little men and women.

The trumpet moved towards the stranger. A boy's voice said:

"Dad, I want you to know that I did not commit suicide.

The coroner said I did, and the jury said I did, but I didn't, Dad. You tried to stop them, but they shut you up."

FATHER: "Yes, that's true. But how did it happen?"

VOICE: "You didn't know I had a gun, did you, Dad? But Mummy did."

FATHER: "Yes, I've found that out since, but how did it happen?"

VOICE (very pathetically): "Well, I was only a boy like other boys, and I wanted to be a highwayman. I took the gun and went out on the by-pass road. Then I tried to shoot a bird, and stumbled and shot myself. That's how it happened. You believe me, don't you, Dad?"

FATHER: "Yes, Teddy boy, I believe you."

VOICE: "Don't cry, Dad, I'm all right now."

It was obvious that his father had difficulty in restraining his tears. When the boy left, Red Cloud said, "That is what they call Beelzebub." The comment was sufficient.

I spoke to the father afterwards. He was very amazed.

"Tell me," I said, "are you sure that it was your boy?"

"Yes," he replied, "that was my boy's voice. They said he committed suicide four months ago, but my wife and I found it difficult to believe it of our son."

Some days later I telephoned to Mrs. Donohoe to ask his name for the purpose of this book. "You must leave his name out," she said.

"Why?" I asked.

"Well, he has been afraid to tell his wife, as she is a Christian Scientist and opposed to Spiritualism."

And yet we wonder why it is hard for Truth to progress.

SIR HENRY SEGRAVE'S RETURN
[22nd January, 1932]

I HAD arranged to take two friends of mine, Mr. and Mrs. Rudolph Mayer, to the voice sitting. In the morning Mr. Mayer telephoned to say his wife had influenza and they were sorry they would be unable to come.

I wondered whether I could take anybody in their place.

Then I remembered that my friend, Hannen Swaffer, had asked me some time ago to take Lady Segrave to a sitting if ever I had an opportunity.

Sir Henry Segrave was interested in Spiritualism. When he was making his attempt at breaking the world's speed record at Daytona Beach in 1927 he received a message given at a séance in England which was of great help to him.

This so aroused his curiosity that on his return to this country he called on Swaffer, whom he knew was interested in Spiritualism.

In his flat he saw some psychic phenomena which impressed him. So much so, that in an article printed in the Sunday Express on the Sunday following his death he was reported as saying, jokingly of course, the only time he was ever frightened was when he saw the piano jump in Hannen Swaffer's flat.

My difficulty now was to get permission for her to be present without mentioning her name. You see I had not asked permission of the guide, the one rigid rule of Red Cloud's sittings.

I telephoned Estelle Roberts and the following dialogue occurred:

M. B.: "Mr. and Mrs. Mayer cannot come tonight as Mrs. Mayer has an attack of influenza. I wonder whether you would mind if I brought a friend in their place?"

ESTELLE ROBERTS: "Have you asked Red Cloud?"

M. B.: "No."

ESTELLE ROBERTS: "Then I am sorry. You know his permission must be asked."

M. B.: "But I am sure he would approve. Anyway, I am prepared to take the responsibility."

After a long argument Mrs. Roberts agreed. I had never met Lady Segrave, but I telephoned and introduced myself to her. I explained the circumstances of the sitting that night, but to my dismay she could not come.

"Where is your friend?" asked Estelle Roberts when I arrived. I explained that my friend was unable to come. I mentioned no names, not even whether it was a man or woman I had intended to bring. In fact, I gave no indication of any kind.

The séance started in the usual way. Out of curiosity I said to Red Cloud: "Do you know anything about the person I tried to bring to-night?"

His reply was very cryptic. "You dry up and wait."

Later on he said to me: "Little man, this is for you." A voice addressed me.

"Barbanell," it called.

"Yes," I replied. "Who is that speaking?"

"Segrave. Thank you for trying to bring my wife."

"That's all right, Sir Henry. I am only sorry she was unable to come."

"No, it is very kind of you. Thank Mr. Swaffer for all his kindness to her, also Mrs. Mayer for letting me speak through her, and also Miss Stead for all she has done."

All this was very evidential. A few weeks previously, he had attempted to speak to Lady Segrave through the mediumship of Mrs. Mayer, but he was so excited, and so was she, that the result was only partially successful. Miss Stead had also been of some assistance to Lady Segrave.

"Sir Henry," I asked, "was it you who returned to Swaffer's flat the Sunday night after your death?"

Yes," came the voice, "that was I."

I asked him for a message for his wife, which he gave. I asked Red Cloud's permission to bring Lady Segrave to the next sitting, which he readily gave.

Immediately the séance was over I telephoned her, told her what had occurred and gave her the message.

A fortnight later I called for her and took her to Estelle Roberts's house. No one present knew her. She was not introduced to the medium.

There were present, of course, three or four sitters who knew she was coming. They had heard my enquiry about bringing her at the last sitting, but I had asked them not to mention this to Mrs. Roberts.

As usual, at the beginning of the séance Red Cloud greeted all his friends present. The trumpet moved towards Lady Segrave and the voice of Red Cloud addressed her. "You don't know me, do you?" he said.

"No," replied Lady Segrave, "I am a stranger here."

"No, you are not. Good evening, Lady Segrave. I will soon bring your little man to you."

The séance continued, several voices carried on long

conversations with their friends present. Soon the trumpet moved towards Lady Segrave.

"D," said a voice. She was so excited, she told me afterwards, that she could not speak. "D" was her nickname.

"D," repeated the voice.

"Speak to him," I whispered. I knew from past experience that the success of a séance depended on the response from the person addressed.

My urging seemed to make her more tense. The trumpet moved towards me. "You are there, Barbanell, aren't you?" said the voice.

"Yes, Sir Henry, but please speak to your wife."

He addressed her by name again. She mumbled a few words and then the trumpet dropped, an indication that Segrave could not hold the "power."

Immediately the voice of Red Cloud was heard. He addressed Lady Segrave.

"You know, little lady, your little man wants to talk to you very much, but you are too tense and he is too excited. I promise you that I will break down the barriers for you, even if I have to do something that is impossible in the attempt, and that is to die."

THE SPIRIT DANCER AND THE CRITIC
[4th March, 1932]

THIS time Hannen Swaffer accompanied me. A few days before, I had a private sitting with Estelle Roberts. Red Cloud said to me, "The Swaffer man wants to sit. Ask him to come on Friday."

This was quite true. Swaffer had mentioned a desire to be present at one of the voice sittings.

There were twenty-two people present at this séance. During the singing of "Onward, Christian soldiers," one of the trumpets moved round the room touching several of the sitters. When it reached Swaffer the voice of Red Cloud was heard saying:

"Welcome, Chief Swaffer;" front line trenches, you."

This was a reference to an extended lecture tour on Spiritualism made by Swaffer in the past three years.

The first spirit voice was Jacky, who greeted his foster-mother, Mrs. L.S. He is one of the regular communicators. His characteristic, thin piping voice is easily distinguished. At these sittings you soon learn to know many of the voices, and you make friendships with people whom you cannot see, and whom you never knew before their passing.

Jacky said: "Mother, we have a little test for you tonight."

He was followed by a voice announcing itself as "Captain Arthur S.," who spoke to Mrs. L.S. I have let her tell her own story.

MRS. L. S.'s STORY

At the direct-voice circle, my usual communicator Jacky only gave me a greeting, as Red Cloud was using his help to bring someone else through. I imagined this might be a woman friend, who had passed over a month before.

Instead, a male voice used the trumpet and gave the name Captain Arthur S—, which I at once recognised.

The conversation was as follows:

VOICE (with difficulty, as if unused to the trumpet): "My name is S—, Captain Arthur S—."

L. S.: "Ah! I think you want to talk to me. I am glad you've come."

VOICE: "Yes" (breathing heavily). "I don't like this thing."

L. S.: "Easier to be in the Army, wasn't it?"

VOICE: "I'd much rather be under orders than try this thing. (The general laughter of the circle gave encouragement and more strength for the communicator to continue.) Now, your brother is going to marry my wife."

L. S.: "Do you approve?

VOICE: "Yes, I do. Tell him to take care of my little girl."

L. S.: "I will. Do you agree that the marriage should take place early?"

VOICE: "Yes. All will be well. (His voice was very firm now.) Tell my wife I am now all right, and that I am sorry about the drink."

L. S.: "Your people have been rather unkind to her about that."

VOICE: "They would hit a man when he is down, you know. Tell my wife I don't like that boat."

L. S.: "She is selling it. Do you advise selling the house too?"

VOICE: "Yes, there are too many old associations. I must go now. You have the name: Captain Arthur S—."

Two days later, I gave the message to the widow. It was interesting to learn that the little yacht which the spirit did not like had been purchased by his widow only after his passing.

Her second marriage took place on 7th April, 1932.

* * *

After the Captain Arthur S— communication, Red Cloud addressed Swaffer:

"Hold on!" he said. "There is an Indian spirit here for you."

A voice announced itself as "White Shadow."

Turning to Swaffer he said, "Thank you for helping my medium. She will soon be ready for the platform."

This was very interesting and evidential. For the past year Swaffer had been sitting with Mr. and Mrs. Mayer, helping in the development of her mediumship.

White Shadow is her guide, and had often said through her that he was training her for public clairvoyance.

Red Cloud, who always speaks between each voice, said, "There is a spirit here who has never spoken before. Will you help him? Hold on!"

A long conversation followed between the voice and a Mrs. Varley. I give Mrs. Varley's own account of what occurred.

MRS. VARLEY'S STORY

The following is an account of a conversation I had with my husband (who passed over in January, 1931) at one of Mrs. Estelle Roberts's direct voice séances.

It was the first of its kind that I had been to and Mrs. Roberts had kindly allowed my aunt to go with me. I had only seen Mrs. Roberts once before, and we were absolute strangers to all the other sitters, all of whom can bear witness to the following conversation.

No one there except Mrs. Roberts (who was in a deep trance all the time and who never spoke once) knew my name—and not even Mrs. Roberts knew my aunt's name. It was the eighth anniversary of my wedding day, and I knew that if it were possible, my husband would get through to me.

For the benefit of anyone who is not a Spiritualist and who may put these things down to imagination or trickery, I should like to say that the room in which the circle was held was quite small.

It was absolutely empty, except for two luminous tin trumpets in the middle of the floor, and the circle of chairs, which were arranged very closely together, and would only just fit into the room.

So much so, that when we were all inside, and the door was shut, some of the sitters were sitting with their chairs against the door, so that nobody could possibly get in or out.

The circle opened with a hymn, during which the medium went into a deep trance. By the time we had reached the last verse, we could see one of the trumpets rise from the floor and float round the room touching different people, and at times soaring up to the ceiling.

Then a strange voice announced itself from the middle of the circle as Red Cloud, Mrs. Roberts's guide. He carried on quite a long conversation with different friends of his amongst the sitters.

His voice was absolutely distinctive and very wonderful.

He told us that there was a great crowd of people there trying to get through to us. He explained that he would speak to us between each one who came so that there should be no question of identities getting mixed.

After that, he called out, "Hold on!" and a different voice started to speak.

Altogether, I should think about a dozen or more different voices came through and carried on long conversations with their various friends and relations giving their names and all sorts of details about their families' lives.

Usually, the trumpet touched the person it wanted, but sometimes it spoke from the ground, almost at their feet, or perhaps from the ceiling.

Often, the conversation was general, and the voice would flash round from one person to another, always picking out just the person it wanted—a thing it would have been impossible for any ordinary person to do, as the room was in complete darkness.

It was all too wonderful for words, and left no room for any doubt. The voices were quite clear and all different. Every one of them was acknowledged.

At last Red Cloud said, "Hold on! There is someone coming through for the first time. I want you all to help. He finds it very difficult. He is full of emotion."

Then the trumpet moved towards me, but about two or three yards away, and a voice whispered, "Dorothy—Dorothy—I want Dorothy."

I leaned forward and called out, "Yes!" To my astonishment, the lady on my left did the same. She turned to me and asked if my name was Dorothy too! However, the whispering continued, growing louder,

"I want Dorothy—I want my wife."

I knew it was for me and that my husband had got through at last. We had been told not to call the voices by name, but to ask who they were. I asked, "Who is it?" His voice grew clearer, and he said, "I'm Bunny, darling. Don't you know me?"

Then we forgot the circle and everybody in the room. We just talked and talked, half the time interrupting each other and speaking at the same time.

There was such a lot to say, and he was so excited.

As far as I can remember, part of the conversation was something like this:

VOICE: "I've been trying so hard to get through. Now at last, at last, but it's so difficult and I can't do it properly."

D. V.: "You're doing it beautifully. I can hear every word."

VOICE: "Do you remember India? And how I went a week ahead of you to get the house ready? Do you remember the flowers I arranged? And the fires? And then—I left you, I left you."

D. V.: "Bunny. You never left me, never."

VOICE: "No, I want you to know that there is no death."

D. V.: "Do you know what day it is?"

VOICE: "Of course I do. As if I'd ever forget—our anniversary. I'll never leave you. I'm always with you. I've been so worried because you tried to come, too. You went out in the cold with nothing on your feet, and I was so frightened. But I was near you and wouldn't let you come. "Promise, promise me that you will never try to come here, because I wouldn't be near you then."

D. V.: "I promise I never will. I know better now."

VOICE: "Yes, it's all right. You're brave now."

D. V.: "How is mother?" (his mother).

VOICE: "She is quite all right; quite happy."

D. V.: "And is Gwennie with you?" (my sister).

VOICE: "Often. She wants to talk to her mother."

D. V.: "Don't go. Are you all right? Are you happy?"

VOICE: "Yes, quite, but I want you. Who is with you? Is that Aunt Dorothy?"

D. V.: "No. Auntie Ethel."

VOICE (addressing my aunt): "Are you Ethel Crosthwaite? You remember me, don't you? I'm Varley."

Then after a few more remarks to me, his voice died down. He had been talking quite loudly, and everyone could hear him. I knew his voice, though it was a bit husky and terribly excited.

Then he gave a whispered, "Oh! I can't do any more." The trumpet fell to the ground.

A moment later Red Cloud called out, "That's a very good test. He is not able to speak well. He is too full of emotion, but he says he went eight days before you to make your home, and in two weeks he died. He was very worried about you trying to come, too."

When Red Cloud had stopped, I thanked him, and he replied, "Don't thank me, thank God."

When my husband referred to Aunt Dorothy (an aunt of his) I think he must have mistaken the sitter on my left for her, as she had spoken to him when he first called out my name. After that, the way he addressed my aunt, giving her name and then his own, was simply wonderful.

They had met only a few times, about eight years ago, as we had been in India since then.

He had spent his Christmas leave with me in 1930, and

insisted on going on a week beforehand to our new station, to get the house ready for us.

When we arrived there on 8th January, 1931, we found that he had unpacked everything and had big fires in all the rooms, as it was bitterly cold.

He had spent most of that day arranging the flowers himself, and had filled the house with them and was very proud of having done everything so beautifully for me.

The next day he contracted pneumonia, and died ten days later.

At first, I thought it would be quite easy for me also to get pneumonia. I tried very hard, even to the extent of walking into the garden at night with no coat on, and with bare feet.

It was frightfully cold at the time. My mother and father, who had arrived by then, had bad colds, but I never even got a cold. After a time I gave up trying to die, as I realised I was being well guarded.

I have written this, hoping that I may help to convince others that there is no such thing as "death," which is just one step further on into Life.

* * *

Amongst those who communicated that night was a young spirit girl named Louise, who frequently speaks to her mother and her aunt. Louise has a very characteristic voice. It rises and falls during every sentence.

Red Cloud has given the best description of her voice. He once said, "Her legs have got into her tongue."

Louise had a conversation with her mother and then spoke to us all.

LOUISE: "They did not tell me when I was on earth that I was a German girl, but it makes no difference here."

HER MOTHER: "Look, Louise, there is Mr. Hannen Swaffer over there. You remember how we used to discuss him."

LOUISE: "Yes, I know. I have been looking at him. You know, Mr. Swaffer, I am afraid of you."

HANNEN SWAFFER: "Why?"

LOUISE: "Well, you see, I am a dancer and you are a critic!"

HANNEN SWAFFER: "That is all right, my dear. It is dark and I cannot see you."

LOUISE (in astonishment): "But I can see you. You must all be dead!" (To her mother.) "Mummy, he is a nice man."

When Louise had gone, a very dramatic happening ensued. Red Cloud called me, told me to pick up the trumpet which was not being used, and to hold it at both ends. I did so.

"There is a man here," he said, "giving the name of Wallace. He is trying to push his way in. He is a dominant personality, but he is not yet ready. He does not know how to use the power and it would harm the medium. (Mrs. Roberts had been ill that week with an attack of influenza.)

"I will bring him through in my own time, but he has to learn that I am master in this house."

At a later séance, Edgar Wallace managed to speak.

"Take care of him, Red Cloud," said Hannen Swaffer. "He is a good sort."

"Yes, but he is very ignorant of these matters," Red Cloud replied. "He wants to speak to you. He says there is a matter he wishes to put right."

"Tell him it is all over now," said Swaffer.

So ended a remarkable séance. I have not attempted to describe all that occurred, but only the outstanding incidents.

It lasted for one and a half hours. There were no pauses of any kind, and at least fifteen separate voices spoke to us.

SIR HENRY SEGRAVE SPEAKS AGAIN
[18th March, 1932]

I HAD brought down with me an old friend of mine named Mrs. K. Fulcher. I had done so because a fortnight earlier Red Cloud had said to me at the last séance, "There is a man here who says he knows you very well; he tells me his name is Fulcher, but you called him "Uncle."

That was quite true.

At the beginning of this séance, Red Cloud asked me to introduce him to Mrs. Fulcher. When I did so, he said to her, "I will soon bring your husband."

Later on the spirit voice of Mr. Fulcher was heard. He gave his name and asked, "Where are you, Kit?" I had known Mr. Fulcher for ten years and it was certainly his voice. "Kit" was evidential, as he always addressed his wife by this nickname.

The following conversation took place:

MRS. FULCHER "Is that you, Alec?"

VOICE: "Yes, where is Barbie?"

(The nickname by which the author is known to his friends.)

M. B.: "I am here, uncle."

VOICE: "Try to make her understand, Barbie; try to help her." Then addressing his wife:

"Don't be sad, Kit. I am always by your side. You are to go on with the work."

MRS. FULCHER "What shall I do about the house?"

VOICE: "You are not to let it. It is too full of memories.

MRS. FULCHER: "You know, Alec, one of your papers is missing. I have not been able to find it."

VOICE: "It was in a desk in the bedroom."

MRS. FULCHER: "I cannot find it."

VOICE: "I will guide you to it."

MRS. FULCHER: "Have you explored much over there?"

VOICE: "Not much. I am always by your side. (Then addressing those present.) Look here, you people, I was a Spiritualist, and I want you all to know that it is far more wonderful over here than ever I had realised."

Then to M. B.:

"Look after her, Barbie. I know she is lonely. I will send someone to stay with her. Don't cry, Kit. Goodbye."

The trumpet now moved to Lady Segrave, and the voice of her husband addressed her.

"I was with you on the 14th, D," he said.

Then followed this conversation:

LADY SEGRAVE: "You remembered the 14th, Boy?"

VOICE: "Your birthday, darling. (To M. B.) Good evening, Barbanell."

M. B.: "Good evening, Sir Henry."

VOICE: "I am trying hard to get through."

LADY SEGRAVE: "Don't go, Boy. Tell me more of yourself."

VOICE: "I knew how to drive a boat, or a car, but I am hanged if I can get the run of this yet.

"I am so much happier since I found you. I will get through again, dear. Do bring her again, Barbanell."

LADY SEGRAVE: "If Red Cloud will let us."

VOICE: "You know perfectly well he will. Can't you push the walls out?"

LADY SEGRAVE: "Can you give me a message for anybody?"

VOICE: "How is mother?"

LADY SEGRAVE: "She has not been well."

VOICE: "I know, but how is she now? You know I have my own mother here."

LADY SEGRAVE: "I wish you would send Bill a message."

VOICE: "Dear old Bill. Is he on the committee of . . .? When is it coming off? Why are they waiting?"

Much more than this was said, but I have suppressed it. He referred to a matter which, Lady Segrave assures me, was known to no one in the world, except herself.

LADY SEGRAVE: "Are you with me in the car, Boy?"

VOICE: "Yes, do take care, D."

LADY SEGRAVE: "Why, I am a very good driver."

VOICE: "Yes, so was I. Good night, darling. Good night, Barbanell."

M. B.: "Good night, Sir Henry."

The whole conversation between Lady Segrave and her husband was very natural. I felt as if I had been eavesdropping. Darkness has some virtue at any rate.

A voice announced itself as "Francis Robert Middleton Phillips." It was claimed by a Mrs. Hankey as her father. Then they spoke to one another.

MRS. HANKEY: "Yes, Father darling. How are you?"

VOICE: "Quite well. I am very busy with Nigel. He is quite all right, so do not worry, Toddles. He will do good business over there with Eric.

"Tell Eric so. How is the trust? Are —** and —** still after that £25, which I lent years ago, and also the money I sent to —** in Canada?"

*** Names and references suppressed by the author.*

MRS. HANKEY: "Yes, Father darling."

VOICE: "Well it is all rubbish. It is nothing to do with the trust. That should be finished, and you have nothing to worry over."

MRS. HANKEY: "I am going away. Shall I go and see John?"

VOICE: "Yes, see John, but you must leave —** You know what they were like to you when I was with you, especially —**. Do you remember I used to sing?"

MRS. HANKEY: "Yes, Father dear." (A voice from the circle.)" Do please sing for us."

VOICE: "I have no time now. I am busy. You have got my ring on, I hope."

MRS. HANKEY: "Yes, Father. What about Tat?"

VOICE: "Just tit for tat. Give my love to Eric. Nigel is quite all right. I will look after him. Goodbye and God bless you."

MRS. HANKEY: "Good night, Father darling."

Mrs. Hankey spoke to Red Cloud and said to him, "Thank you so much, Red Cloud."

His reply to that was his usual, "Don't thank me, I am but the instrument. Thank God."

Here again, many names and details of family matters have been deleted. They might pain people still alive. Mrs. Hankey assured me—and she ought to know—that every fact was right.

** *Names and references suppressed by the author.*

MRS. SWAFFER AND HER SISTER-IN-LAW.
SPIRIT VOICE DICTATES TO SHORTHAND WRITER
[1st April, 1932]

SIR HENRY SEGRAVE was almost the first spirit to speak. The trumpet moved close to Lady Segrave and rested in her lap. Then followed this conversation:

VOICE: "D. It is Boy."

LADY SEGRAVE: "How are you, Boy"

VOICE: "Quite all right, darling."

LADY SEGRAVE: "I have a message for you from your father." This she gave.

VOICE: "Tell my father to come here and speak. Did you give my message to Bill?"

LADY SEGRAVE.: "No, I have not seen him. Have you sent me any messages in the last fortnight, darling?"

VOICE: "Yes, through the—woman."

Here he named a certain medium.

LADY SEGRAVE: "No, I don't mean that."

VOICE: "Oh dear, I have to put up with such a lot! How are you?"

Lady Segrave had had several messages sent to her by various people. These, they alleged, emanated from her husband, but none of them was evidential.

Whenever celebrities pass on, there are many foolish Spiritualists who claim to get messages from them.

LADY SEGRAVE: "I am much better. Do you know about all my troubles in the early days?"

VOICE: "Yes. Have you got my coat on tonight?"

LADY SEGRAVE: "No, not tonight. But I do wear it."

VOICE: "I know, I know. You wear it when you take the dog out."

LADY SEGRAVE: "Yes, I always say, 'This is Father's coat.'"

VOICE: "Good evening, Swaffer."

HANNEN SWAFFER: "So glad to hear from you, de Hane."

VOICE: "Thank you for all you did."

HANNEN SWAFFER: "There is no need to thank me."

VOICE "But there is. After all you showed me the way to truth."

HANNEN SWAFFER: "Well, you started it on earth, you know."

VOICE: "I knew a little. There is one thing I would like to say; don't let her go to too many mediums."

HANNEN SWAFFER: "I quite understand, and I shall advise her about your case. I am sure she will take my advice."

LADY SEGRAVE "It is rather tempting, you know."

VOICE: "It is all right provided you go in the right direction. (To M. B.) You know the dross from the gold."

This referred to a "séance" I had had with a fraudulent medium, whom I exposed. I even tried to obtain a warrant for his arrest, but my application was unsuccessful.

HANNEN SWAFFER: "This is Mrs. Swaffer, de Hane. She wants to speak to you."

VOICE: "I have sent you a message through White Shadow. (The guide of Mrs. Mayer.) I am delighted to see you. I will help you in any way I can. I know your sister quite well." (Mrs. Swaffer's "dead" sister spoke later on.)

HANNEN SWAFFER "You must try and help Wallace."

VOICE: "Yes, but I do not know very much. (To Lady Segrave.) I put you there tonight, I wanted you to sit there."

Before each circle, the sitters' psychic "powers" are "balanced" by Estelle Roberts, under Red Cloud's influence, who tells each one where to sit. Lady Segrave had been moved from her usual seat and placed nearer the medium.

LADY SEGRAVE: "Yes, it is wonderful. You are absolutely sitting with me."

VOICE: "Tell my father to come here."

LADY SEGRAVE: "He is rather deaf."

VOICE: "Tell him I will shout like the deuce. Good night, God bless you. Good night, everybody."

Red Cloud then addressed Mrs. Swaffer:

"Your sister is here, and I hope she does not run away when she speaks." Then there came a voice.

"Lottie," it said.

To my knowledge, Lottie generally appears at séances whenever Mrs. Swaffer or Hannen Swaffer is present. I never knew her on earth, but I know her now.

Through various mediums she has built up a personality which I can easily recognise.

She is always quietly unassuming, very retiring, and it is difficult to get her to speak.

This was the first occasion on which she had spoken at the voice séance. Immediately she announced herself, the trumpet, which is made of aluminium and is in two parts, collapsed and fell to the floor.

Invisible hands picked up the pieces and put them together again.

Then Lottie made another effort. Here is the conversation which took place:

MRS. SWAFFER: "Is that you, dear? Come along."

VOICE (almost in a whisper): "I am quite close to you."

MRS. SWAFFER: "Speak a little louder if you can."

VOICE: "I will try. I am so happy, dear, I want to thank you for what you did for John." (Her nephew.)

MRS. SWAFFER: "Are you pleased about it, dear? Is he going to be all right?"

VOICE: "That is why I made an effort to come. I tried last time when Freddie was here. I am quite close to you."

This is very evidential. She always called Hannen Swaffer "Freddie." Few people know his full name.

MRS. SWAFFER: "If you would talk a little louder I could hear you better."

HANNEN SWAFFER: "I think you are very good, Lot."

VOICE: "It sounds as though I am shrieking."

(When the voices are faint and we tell them so, they always seem astonished. They usually say they are shouting.)

"I have had it out with Wallace and he is penitent."

(This refers to a curious experience recorded by Edgar Wallace in the Sunday News in May, 1931. He had become its editor and had written several attacks on Swaffer.

In one issue he recorded how, after he had written some more paragraphs attacking Swaffer, he left his study. On returning he found his paragraphs missing.

The paper on which they were written had disappeared.

Then to his surprise, he saw sitting in a chair a woman, whom he recognised as Swaffer's sister-in-law.

She told him not to be so silly and to stop his attacks on Swaffer.

Edgar Wallace was obviously a psychic, otherwise this could not have happened. Anyway, it impressed him, for he ended his article by saying, "I shall never sneer at spirits again."

Lottie's reference to Wallace is, therefore, rather striking.)

HANNEN SWAFFER: "We don't want penitence. I knew you would help him. He is a very fine chap, you know."

VOICE: "Just like you, Freddie."

HANNEN SWAFFER: "I thought it was awfully nice of Wallace to write all that down."

VOICE: "I knew he was coming here, but was not allowed to say so. He does so want to speak to his wife."

HANNEN SWAFFER: "What does he want her to do, Lot?"

VOICE: "He wants her to realise he can never forget her and the children."

HANNEN SWAFFER: "Well, he had worries and troubles in the past, and he always got over them."

VOICE: "Yes, but remember he loves his wife and children."

HANNEN SWAFFER: "You always come along to the Mayers, don't you, Lot?"

VOICE: "Yes. Will you bring John here, shortly, dear?"

HANNEN SWAFFER: "I know Red Cloud would like John."

VOICE: "If I am allowed to, I will come then. He let me through tonight."

HANNEN SWAFFER: "We are always talking about you, Lot dear."

VOICE: "I am always with you. Take care of yourself, dear, and don't worry about me."

MRS. SWAFFER "The children know you are guiding

them."

VOICE: "I was quite close to you yesterday when you were talking to John."

HANNEN SWAFFER: "YOU must help him."

VOICE: "Of course I will, but what am I when there are all these great guides?"

HANNEN SWAFFER: "We would rather have you, Lot."

VOICE: "That is why the guides send us. Good night. God bless you."

RED CLOUD (to Swaffer): "She saw all the people and ran away."

HANNEN SWAFFER: "She was always like that."

MRS. SWAFFER: "Thank you, Red Cloud."

RED CLOUD: "Don't thank me, thank God. Look what your little man has done for us. We always pay for service."

Then there came another voice. Here is a record of what was said:

VOICE: "Father, this is Helen."

SITTER: "Yes, Helen. How are you?

VOICE (to circle): "Dad always called me Isabel.

Have you my bell in your pocket?"

SITTER: "Yes; you ring it sometimes."

VOICE: "Auntie Joan is here tonight. Give her my love. What is that lady doing behind the curtain?"

(When I first attended these voice séances I was so struck with their evidential quality, that I asked permission to have a stenographer present to record all the conversations.

Previous experience has taught me that unless they are recorded at the time, a great deal of valuable evidence is lost.

Red Cloud readily agreed to my suggestion. An alcove in the room was partitioned off and a stenographer recorded the conversations at every séance.)

M. B.: "Taking down notes."

VOICE: "Does she want details? (The trumpet moved towards the alcove.) I am Helen Isabel Hatfield. I was electrocuted by a fan. I fainted and fell on a fan. I was a Girl Guide."

SITTER: "Yes, the captain."

VOICE: "Winnie, my sister, wears my uniform. Is that what you want?"

M. B.: "Yes."

VOICE: "They all forgot father's birthday and I reminded them, but he did not share his presents."

M. B.: "How did you remind them?"

VOICE: "I told them."

HANNEN SWAFFER: "That is the advantage of being a Girl Guide."

VOICE (to Swaffer): "I like your face."

HANNEN SWAFFER: "It's all right in the dark."

VOICE: "But it is not dark to us. You are the ones in darkness. Give my love to Mother."

SITTER: "And Mother sends lots to you. Goodbye."

THE AMUSING SPIRIT
[15th April, 1932]

MY friends, Mr. and Mrs. Mayer, who were unable to come to the séance on 22nd January, came with me to this sitting.

After the usual preliminaries, Red Cloud greeted us with "God bless you all. You can loose hands."

Mrs. Treloar explained: "Red Cloud means he has faith in you not to interfere with the trumpets or the phenomena in any way."

RED CLOUD: "No, they would not do that. They would not kill the goose that lays the golden eggs. Good evening to all. (To Hannen Swaffer.) Good evening, Chief. How is the squaw?"

HANNEN SWAFFER: "Better, thanks. I think she likes her treatment very much. It is very good of you."

(Red Cloud's healing forms an important part of his work. Through his medium he has trained several people who constitute his band of psychic healers. Mrs. Swaffer was having healing treatment.)

RED CLOUD: "It is very good of you to help us. My brother White Shadow is here. He is a very solid shadow. I am very happy to see you, Mayer lady."

MRS. MAYER: "I am very happy to be here."

RED CLOUD: "Is this the first time you have heard my voice?"

MRS. MAYER: "Yes."

RED CLOUD: "Not nervous, are you?"

MRS. MAYER: "No, I am very happy."

RED CLOUD (to Lady Segrave): "Your chief is doing good work."

LADY SEGRAVE: "Is he going to speak to me?"

RED CLOUD: "I hope so. Hold on"

This was the conversation between the next spirit voice and a sitter:

VOICE: "Betty. I want Betty."

SITTER: "Yes, what do you want?"

VOICE: "I am Avery."

BETTY: "How nice to hear you."

VOICE: "Alan is here."

BETTY: Both of you there; how wonderful!"

VOICE: "Harry Harding is here."

BETTY: "Is he there too? His mother will be interested."

VOICE: "He so wanted his mother."

BETTY: "Have you a message for Father and Mother, Ave?"

VOICE: "I am so happy to get here. Don't worry about India."

BETTY: "Is it all right there?"

VOICE: "Yes. He will get what you want him to get soon."

BETTY: "Another time I shall hear you more distinctly."

VOICE: "I am trying so hard. Do not allow anyone to spoil your ideas."

BETTY: "No, I won't, Ave."

VOICE: "Keep straight on. Tell Lady —** her two boys are here, George and Harry."

BETTY: "I will. How is Alan?"

VOICE: "Alan is with me, dear. He hopes to speak to you

** *Names and references suppressed by the author.*

at some time."

BETTY: "I am delighted to hear you, Ave."

VOICE: "I will look after your future."

BETTY: "I'm so glad."

VOICE: "Tell Willoughby that his post in India will improve shortly. Encourage him. He misses you."

BETTY: "Shall I go to India, Ave, in the autumn?"

VOICE: "I don't think so. You have the boy and the girl to think of."

BETTY: "But I have not got a boy and girl."

VOICE: "You have looked after a little boy and girl who have a great worry."

BETTY: "Oh yes —** I know."

VOICE: "I will help you. Give my love to Mother."

BETTY: "I will. But she will not believe it."

VOICE: "I know. Alan sends his love. We two brothers are always together."

"Good night and God bless you."

This sitter assured me that the whole of the conversation teemed with evidence that she understood perfectly. Red Cloud, as usual, immediately followed.

"Try and help this next little lady," he said. "Encourage her. Don't give anything away, but just encourage her. It is strange for her."

(Red Cloud is always keen on making his séances evidential, hence his constant warning not to give information away.

It requires a little practice to learn how to encourage and stimulate the voices, without disturbing the evidential value of the communications.)

The following conversation then took place:

VOICE: "Can you hear me? Gertrude, I am Gertrude Lodge. Norman!"

NORMAN: "God bless you, darling."

VOICE: "I am your daughter. I wanted to hear your voice."

NORMAN: "You are doing so well."

VOICE: "Willie is here."

NORMAN: "Well done. I am so glad."

(Notice that it is the spirit who gives the names, which often the sitters have forgotten.)

VOICE: "Tom and Charlie are here. They are trying to help you, dear."

NORMAN: "That is very good of them."

VOICE: "Are you feeling happy?"

NORMAN: "Yes. Did you see me today?"

VOICE: "Yes. When you went to the city?"

NORMAN: "Oh, yes I did, but I did not mean that."

VOICE: "But I do. How is Mabel?"

NORMAN: "Shall I give her your love?"

VOICE: "Yes, and Martha. I am so glad to come here. You have come a long way."

NORMAN: "Yes, it is a long way."

VOICE: "I know you are going down to Kent. When are you going?"

NORMAN: "Sunday."

VOICE: "Give them both my love there. The place is in a mess."

NORMAN: "I dare say that is true. I will find out on Sunday."

VOICE: "Will you kiss the babies for me? I don't find it so easy to get into your new room."

NORMAN: "My new room?"

VOICE: "Yes, you have changed your bedroom."

NORMAN: "Well, I am not aware of it. Perhaps I shall be when I get back."

VOICE: "God bless you. Come again."

Red Cloud then addressed the sitter.

"Is it close to an anniversary?" he asked.

NORMAN: "Yes, very close, Red Cloud."

RED CLOUD: "She could not get it through. She dropped the trumpet. It is very near—three days."

NORMAN: "Quite right, Red Cloud."

Then there came the following conversation:

VOICE: "It is Annie speaking. I want Emily. Sarah, it is Annie Mason. Take my thimble out of your bag."

SARAH: "Do you want me to take it out?"

VOICE: "No, I only wanted you to know it is me. She always has my thimble. (This was said to the other sitters.) Charlie is here."

(A long conversation followed concerning a story that the sitter was receiving "inspirationally." The spirit voice knew all about it and gave some advice.)

RED CLOUD "Hold on! Still they come. These are the dead ones!"

HANNEN SWAFFER: "Yes, Red Cloud. They are the 'dead' ones."

M. B.: "I am afraid we are the dead ones."

RED CLOUD: "When are you going to bring young John?" (Swaffer's nephew.)

HANNEN SWAFFER "When you invite him."

RED CLOUD: "I ask him now. We try to render service all the time to those who render service. Hold on! Try and help this boy."

VOICE: "Oppie."

SITTER: "Are you going to speak in Dutch or English?"

VOICE: "I am trying to talk. Can you hear me? Is H—** here?

SITTER: "No."

VOICE (sadly): "It is a pity."

SITTER: "You have not forgotten your English."

VOICE: "I try to keep a contact. Tell —** it is not necessary to bring my ashes from Paris."

SITTER: "You promised to tell me this morning."

VOICE: "I keep my promises. I like the young medium."

SITTER: "He is very fat, is he not?"

VOICE: "He is very difficult for us to use."

SITTER: "He wants to be used very much."

VOICE: "Will you do your best to help him?"

SITTER: "Certainly, we will."

VOICE: "My love to Father and to Mother. God bless you."

RED CLOUD: "That is the first time he has got through plainly."

SITTER "He started to tell me last time in Dutch, but broke down after two or three words."

RED CLOUD: "It is better to get it through the instrument in English. Hold on! There is a guide coming."

At a previous séance, this spirit boy wrote a complete letter in Dutch on a blackboard.

(Running Water, a guide, who had already given proof of his identity to his medium elsewhere, gave him some advice.)

RED CLOUD: "He managed all right."

HANNEN SWAFFER: "He has a very good laugh."

RED CLOUD: "Shall I laugh for you? (He did so.) The

** *This name, although given and recognised by the sitter, was not understood by the stenographer.*

doctor said, 'That is not a laugh, it's a bellow!'"

(Red Cloud often refers to the spirit doctors who work with him. They include some well-known English medical men who have passed on. Several of their names are known to me.)

HANNEN SWAFFER: "How is the case going on?" (A law case involving a medium was then before the court.)

RED CLOUD: "You know, Chief, if they did not believe the Nazarene, whom will they believe?

"They have Moses and the Prophets. If they believe not Moses nor the Prophets, neither will they believe if one rose from the dead. It is not going to be easy for her even now."

HANNEN SWAFFER "We have got to go on fighting, anyway."

RED CLOUD: Go on, Chief. Red Cloud is going on until the end."

HANNEN SWAFFER "We are only entitled to the progress we make. It is our own fault."

RED CLOUD "The laws teach you, only you all forget. Ask and ye shall receive. Seek and ye shall find. Knock and the door will be opened to you. Those that mourn are comforted. I send unto you the Comforter. Hold on! This one has got the trumpet. I am letting her in to keep her quiet."

The spirit who spoke was an amusing communicator. The dialogue is recorded exactly as spoken. It is a pity that her mannerisms and intonations cannot be reproduced.

VOICE: "I am hunting for my buttons."

SITTER: "You don't want buttons on that side."

VOICE: "We have to put buttons on our clothes."

SITTER: "You have not got very far, then."

VOICE: "Well, where do you think I have got?"

** *This name, although given and recognised by the sitter, was not understood by the stenographer.*

SITTER: "What about that cheque?

VOICE: "What did you do with it?

SITTER: "Well, fancy having a cheque for thirty years and expecting to cash it!"

VOICE: "What about my dresses? You burned them!"

SITTER: "They were so ugly. Was it you who turned the electric light on the other day? Well, don't do it. I have to pay for it."

VOICE: "So did I have to pay for the frocks. Do you remember that wine I put in the bottle?"

SITTER: "Why did you do that?"

VOICE: "Just to annoy you. Why did you take all the plants out of my garden?"

SITTER: "They did not bloom."

VOICE: "Why did you burn Father's coat?"

SITTER: "I did not know the money was in it. You hid your money from Father, and Father hid his from you."

VOICE: "I am sorry you had to pay the bread bill."

SITTER: "Yes. Fancy letting it run up as much as that. £13 for bread and flour!"

VOICE: "Jim promised to help me."

SITTER: "He did, but you ran it up again."

VOICE: "Did you bring the feather bed away?"

SITTER: "Yes, one of them."

VOICE: "What did you do with the others?"

SITTER: "They were so bad, the old rag and bone man would not take them away."

VOICE: "I am going out now. Goodbye."

RED CLOUD: "That has helped her more than anything. Hold on!"

This conversation shows that after "death," spirits retain

their idiosyncrasies. Our experiences prove that death produces no immediate change in character.

There were several other long conversations between spirit voices and their friends, messages of a personal nature which I cannot record here.

Sir Henry Segrave spoke again. His voice was stronger and he spoke with greater ease. He revealed a knowledge of all that was happening around Lady Segrave.

When she asked him, "Were you at the little house last night, Boy?" he replied, "Yes. You had a lady with you."

LADY SEGRAVE: "It was Barbara. Do you remember her?"

VOICE: "Yes. How is she? By the way, D, you had an awful lot of dogs there. They kept running in between my legs."

Lady Segrave told me this was very evidential. Her friend had brought three dogs with her.

Red Cloud greeted Mr. and Mrs. Mayer.

"Is Spread Eagle here?" she asked. Spread Eagle is her husband's guide, who has often spoken through her in trance.

RED CLOUD: "Yes."

HANNEN SWAFFER: "We would like to hear him."

RED CLOUD (to Mr. Mayer): "You have a brother over here."

MR. MAYER: "Yes, I have."

RED CLOUD: "He has just said to me, 'Do you think I can speak to my brother through that?' (the trumpet). He has been over some time. Hold on! A guide coming."

The trumpet floated until it touched the ceiling. It moved round the circle and touched the five people present, who were all members of Mrs. Mayer's circle.

A loud voice greeted us. "Spread Eagle," it shouted. I

recognised the voice, for Spread Eagle had often spoken to me through the mediumship of Mrs. Mayer.

Red Cloud, as usual, immediately followed. Addressing Hannen Swaffer he said: "Lottie (Swaffer's sister-in-law) is here tonight, Chief. She stood back."

HANNEN SWAFFER: "She always stands back. I hope you have tried to help Wallace!"

RED CLOUD: "Yes, and Segrave has been trying to help him. He can talk to him better than I can. God bless you all."

SIR HENRY SEGRAVE AND THE EARL OF COTTENHAM
[13th May, 1932]

JUST as the circle was about to begin, one of the sitters complained of feeling unwell and had to leave. This meant, of course, disturbing the whole circle, and I was afraid the results would be poor. Nevertheless, it was an excellent sitting and evidence, as usual, poured through.

A fortnight before, Lady Segrave had asked Red Cloud whether she could bring a friend. She mentioned no name. When he arrived, she did not introduce him to Estelle Roberts or to any of the sitters.

He was the Earl of Cottenham, an old friend of Segrave's, who soon greeted him.

"Hallo, D," he said first of all. Then, to Lord Cottenham, "Hullo, Mark."

Lord Cottenham told me afterwards, Segrave always called him "Mark."

LORD COTTENHAM: "Hullo, old boy. Will you tell me something?"

VOICE: "If I can."

LORD COTTENHAM "Am I working on the right lines? I mean, is the idea at the back of my mind a sound one?"

VOICE: "Yes, I think so."

LORD COTTENHAM: "Can you give me a hand with it?"

VOICE: "I am going to."

HANNEN SWAFFER: "You are doing fine now, de Hane.

We are always glad to see you."

VOICE: "I have been afraid for D."

LORD COTTENHAM: "She is happier than she has been for ages."

(Here again I have deleted some of the conversation.)

HANNEN SWAFFER: We are gradually roping them all in."

VOICE: "I think it is just great—can you tell me how to work this thing?" (the trumpet).

HANNEN SWAFFER: "Put your mouth to the hole and talk."

VOICE: "But tell me first where is the hole?"

HANNEN SWAFFER: "You are happier than you were that night."

VOICE: "Ask yourself, Swaffer. Don't you realise that this, even as it is, has made me so? I did not want to leave her.

"As you know, we had all our early struggles together, and just as success came, this happened. I accepted it for myself, but not for D."

LORD COTTENHAM: "D is much happier than you think, old lad. We are looking after her all we can. She is especially happy since she has been here to talk to you."

VOICE: " Stick to it, D. Success in the end. Give my love to —**."

LADY SEGRAVE: "I am having dinner with . . on Monday and I will tell him, but he won't believe me."

VOICE: "Thank God, Mark has got some common sense. —** is a good sort, isn't he?"

LORD COTTENHAM: "Yes, bless his heart."

VOICE: "But as dull as ditch-water! Thank the lady who gave you this privilege." (the medium).

*** Names and references suppressed by the author.*

LORD COTTENHAM: "One more thing before you go. You know I am thinking of writing a rather long book, and I have asked D to help me, as a matter of course. Do you wish that?"

VOICE: "That is just what I want her to do."

LORD COTTENHAM: "All right, old boy. Good night."

A male voice spoke to a Mrs. Liddell, who was present. It belonged to a doctor, whom she knew on earth. He is now assisting Red Cloud in his healing.

"B. G.," as he called himself, gave Mrs. Liddell a great deal of information. His voice was perfectly natural and his sense of humour very well developed.

Here is an extract from the conversation:

MRS. LIDDELL: "You know I am going to talk to you on Thursday."

VOICE: "I am perfectly aware of it."

MRS. LIDDELL: Do you know what day it is?"

VOICE: "The anniversary of my death."

MRS. LIDDELL: "Have you anything to say about Michael?"

VOICE: "No. I am quite satisfied."

MRS. LIDDELL "Is he quite happy at school?"

VOICE: "Yes. There is a gentleman over there I wish to speak to."

The trumpet moved to one of the sitters and "B. G." gave him some advice about his health.

As an example of a perfect communication, here is a record of the conversation between Lady Carey and her "voice."

VOICE: "Betty. It is Alan. How are you, dear?"

LADY CAREY: "All right, thank you."

VOICE: "Avery is here. I am trying to speak."

LADY CAREY: How is Willoughby"

VOICE: "Very well. I have been to India to see him. Listen, dear, you will get a big surprise from Willoughby soon."

LADY CAREY: "Something nice?"

VOICE: "Yes. I am very glad to have come."

LADY CAREY: "I am so glad to hear you again."

VOICE: "I have not been here before. It is Avery who comes here. Don't worry about Willoughby. You tell them about Avery, don't you?"

LADY CAREY: "Yes."

VOICE: "You have sent Willoughby some reading matter."

LADY CAREY: "Yes."

VOICE: "Please send him some more."

LADY CAREY "Am I doing all right?"

VOICE: "It is a wonderful success to get Willoughby to listen to the spirit. He is man of the world. I like the girls. They are two nice girls."

LADY CAREY: "Yes, you would like them if you were here."

VOICE: "I wish I was on the earth."

LADY CAREY: "You were always a great boy for the girls."

VOICE: "I still am. It is a treat to come to you. I wish I could give my love to Mother."

LADY CAREY: "I will try and make her understand."

VOICE: "It makes me think of the Irishman. I am alive and I am dead."

HANNEN SWAFFER "You can't die for the life of you!"

Lady Carey told me that "Alan" was her brother, and "Willoughby" was her husband.

The two girls he referred to were being chaperoned by her through the season.

The next two "voices" spoke to a Colonel Swayne. They were both very natural. The first one announced himself as "Val."

COL. SWAYNE: "Hullo, old man. It is good of you to come."

VOICE: "I am trying so hard to get through this jolly old thing."

COL. SWAYNE: "You are doing well for the first time."

VOICE: "That is what I thought. I have tried before, but it escaped me. Carry on. I will be with you next time. Carry on."

COL. SWAYNE: "Cheerio."

VOICE: "I did not say, ' Cheerio.' I said, ' Carry on.

He was immediately followed by a lady's voice announcing itself as Louisa Swayne."

COL. SWAYNE: "You've come again, Mother. This is so good of you."

VOICE: "I wanted to practise. Did you speak to Val? I pushed him in."

COL. SWAYNE: "Thank you so much."

VOICE: "I am so happy to come, dear."

COL. SWAYNE: "You are speaking so well."

VOICE: "I hope to help you all I can. It is such a long time since I came here, about fifteen years."

COL. SWAYNE: "Yes, nearly sixteen years."

VOICE "But I am not dead, dear."

COL. SWAYNE: "I know that, but you knew about this before you passed over."

VOICE: "Yes, it helped me. I am so glad to come here. Can you hear me? I want to get perfect in this."

There was a lot more, but this book is not the place to

record what was said.

I asked Lord Cottenham to read this chapter and here are his comments.

BY THE EARL OF COTTENHAM

I have read the conversation which, jointly with Lady Segrave, Hannen Swaffer and Maurice Barbanell, I held with Sir Henry Segrave on this evening. Although fragmentary, and perhaps on that account unsatisfying to the general reader, it is accurate to the best of my knowledge, memory and belief.

When studying these conversations, it must, I think, be borne in mind that in cold print they suffer not only because the little humours, the characteristic tones and inflections, the simple naturalness of the communicator's voice is lost, but also because connecting sentences, expressions and phrases have necessarily been deleted, as being too private for publication.

This particular talk was by no means the most intimate or instructive that I have had with Sir Henry, since his death on Lake Windermere. It is included here merely because it was the first, and for that reason might be considered more interesting than any other conversation I have recently held with him.

I have publicly affirmed, and here I do so again, that I have no reasonable doubt of the genuineness of these psychic communications. After patient and searching investigation, such common sense and logic as I possess can find no other explanation than that I have actually conversed with friends and relatives whose physical bodies I know to be dead.

Of what often passes for Spiritualism there is, and rightly

should be, much criticism. Of true Spiritualism, as I have been privileged to encounter it, there can be none, for it brings to light and life the pure teaching of Jesus Christ.

That among professed Spiritualists there are vain, quarrelsome people, mountebanks, vapid, neurotic women, blasphemous, fraudulent fortune-tellers and crooks, no one can deny. But beneath this covering of money-making hypocrisy there is an infinitely comforting truth, free to all who seek it.

One of these days the great newspapers may think it worth their while to send earnest, accredited reporters in search of it to print what they find, ungarbled, to let this truth stand out on their news-sheets, unsullied by any unprincipled penny-a-liner, incapable of recognising truth, or of owning to it if he does.

One of these days, too, the established churches will probe also. They will have to, or they will continue to lose their influence. They will have to probe deeply and withhold none of their findings, or they will become inept even more quickly than now.

One of these days Spiritualists themselves will have to purge their ranks, drastically, and in the sight of all men. For their bogus members are an offence to right-thinking men and women of all religions and degrees of faith.

Nothing can stifle Truth—nothing at all. Public opinion, newspapers that misdirect it, churches, scientists, even Spiritualists themselves will not in the long run hide, distort, belittle or exaggerate the basic truth that a holy communion is possible with those who have passed into the next world and left us wondering.

The study of this means of communication is of the very

first importance to the peoples of this earth.

It should be undertaken whenever possible by all reputable people who are not afraid to relate what they feel, hear and see. In other words, by all who really believe in God. For one of the manifestations of God is truth, and I hold that no investigation of any problem, material or psychic, conducted with faith in Him and an honest desire to serve humanity, can possibly be harmful. Knowledge of some kind will result. And by knowledge alone, which comes like everything else from God, can man tell good from evil.

THE JAPANESE SPEED BOAT VICTIM
[29th April, 1932]

THE first spirit voice to address us, after Red Cloud had opened the circle, was Jacky.

He was followed by a spirit calling himself "Peter Hadfield." You will notice how the spirit corrected us, when we repeated some of the names incorrectly.

VOICE: "This is Peter Hadfield. I have never spoken before."

SITTER: "Are you Charlie's brother?"

VOICE: "Yes, of course I am. I am here with Jarvis."

SITTER: "Jervis?"

VOICE (very emphatically): "No, Jarvis."

SITTER: "How wonderful! Is Jarvis with you?"

VOICE: "Yes, we came together. We have brought him through for the first time. They will be pleased to know. Tell the others."

SITTER: "Yes. I will write to them tomorrow."

VOICE: "Tell them I have met Jean."

SITTER: "Jane?"

VOICE: "No! Jean, JEAN, JEAN! And her little daughter. Good night, dear."

A very striking incident happened that night. There had been several conversations between the voices and some sitters. Red Cloud, as usual, had addressed us between each voice. Then he said:

"There is a young man here. I am going to help him. Hold

on."

The voice spoke to a Mrs. Yano, who was present.

VOICE: "I am Shinji, Shinji Yano. I say, Dulce!"

MRS. YANO: "Oh! Yes. What have you to say?"

VOICE: "Segrave brought me here."

MRS. YANO: "Thank him for me."

VOICE: "We are both together, my brother and I. I do not want Haro to grieve always."

MRS. YANO: "I know."

VOICE: "He saw me die in that boat."

MRS. YANO: "Yes, I know."

VOICE: "Yes, but we got the speed. Haro must take his university examination in December."

MRS. YANO: "How can I make them understand in Japan that I must stay here until the end of the year?"

VOICE: "Tell them Kingi and I said so. Look, dear, I want you to render my thanks and your thanks to Sir Henry when he comes.

"There is a well-known man here in your midst," Segrave says. (To Swaffer.) "I was one who gave my life for speed. I was so sorry that Haro saw me die."

MRS. YANG: "Yes, I know."

VOICE: "It is hard to make you understand that it is like a premature birth when you pass like that."

MRS. YANO: "Yes, I have read a lot lately, and Haro will try to understand."

VOICE: "He is a good boy, Dulce."

MRS. YANO: "Yes, and he will realise this knowledge more and more."

VOICE: "Give my love to the girls."

MRS. YANO: "They put some flowers at the little shrine.

Betty always offers some flowers."

VOICE: "Yes, I know. I saw them. Tell Lady Segrave that her husband is doing some good work. He has helped me. Good night. Kingi says he will try and come next time."

Mrs. Dulce Yano is a sister-in-law of Shingi Yano, who was killed on 29th August, 1929, while practising in a motor-boat at Bury Lake, Rickmansworth, for a Daily Mirror trophy.

Here is Mrs. Yano's account of the sitting.

MRS. D. YANO'S STORY

A week before the accident in which Shingi Yano lost his earthly life, he and my husband, Kingi Yano, were giving the boat a trial. My husband, who used to race at Brooklands, was driving.

He turned the wheel much too suddenly and almost upset the boat. That experience seemed to give him a great shock, and he prophesied that that kind of speed racing must result in some terrible accident. Shingi pooh-poohed the suggestion and laughingly remarked, "Well, if I do go before you, I will come and meet you. In any case, I will let you know all about it."

The following week, the accident he had prophesied happened.

The tragedy upset my husband very much. He was some years older than his brother and had sponsored the trials on the boat. He felt more or less responsible for his brother's passing. My husband was then just getting over a serious illness. Two sports that had been forbidden him by the doctors were golf and fast motor-driving.

While Shingi was there, he gave up those sports, but as his restraining influence was no longer felt, he again indulged in them. He caught a chill and five months later he passed.

My husband's body was cremated and I took his ashes to Japan. On the journey I met a Spiritualist. I spoke to her quite a lot, and she urged me to seek comfort in Spiritualism, but at that time I was far too stricken with grief even to think about it.

On the way back, strangely enough, I became friendly with another Spiritualist. I attended some public Spiritualist meeting, where I received some evidential messages.

In Japan we remember anniversaries every month, and 29th April was an anniversary of Shingi's passing. On this day, I went to a direct-voice séance at Mrs. Roberts's home at Teddington. Several voices had spoken and then Red Cloud said, "Hold on. There is a young man here. I am going to help him." I felt this must be Shin and a moment later he came through.

The voice was Shin's own, and he had the same manner-isms as when he was with us here. He invariably prefixed his remarks with "I say," and almost the first thing he said was, "I say, Dulce."

I could hardly believe my ears when he announced his name, "Shingi Yano," but then he repeated it louder and more clearly.

The reference to Sir Henry Segrave was very interesting, as both he and Shingi lost their lives in speed boats, and were known to one another on earth.

My son, Haro, was very grief-stricken after the accident, and it interfered greatly with his studies.

Shingi had set his heart on achieving a certain speed at the trial run. My husband was timing him. One lap had just been finished and he was at the beginning of another when the boat overturned.

His statement was correct. He achieved his speed.

A NIGHT OF EVIDENCE
[27th May, 1932]

AMONG the first to speak was a young girl who spoke to her father and mother. You could hear that the voice belonged to someone of Scottish birth.

She gave her name without hesitation:

VOICE: "Mother, it is Helen speaking."

SITTER: "Come along, darling."

VOICE: "It is Helen Macleod speaking. Where is Father? Speak to me."

FATHER: "Yes, dear. What is it?"

VOICE: "Father, take my watch off your arm."

FATHER: "Do you want me to, dear?"

VOICE: "I am only trying to tell you it is there."

FATHER: "Yes, it is very clever of you. It is there."

VOICE (to mother): "You have my ring on your finger."

MOTHER: "Yes, darling."

VOICE: "Mother, can you not hear me, dear?"

MOTHER: "Not very well."

VOICE: "I am quite close to you. Is that clearer?"

MOTHER: "Yes. What do you want to tell me? Come along, darling."

VOICE: "I am coming with you to the ' Hand.' You know— (there was a pause, then very deliberately) you know, the Reflectograph."

(The Reflectograph is a fairly recent method invented to obtain spirit communication. It consists of a large keyboard, all the letters being very delicately balanced.

A materialised hand is seen to depress the keys, which enable illuminated letters to be flashed on to a screen.)

MOTHER: "That is tomorrow."

VOICE: "Wake yourself up!"

MOTHER: "That is very like you, Helen. Tell us more. We have come a long way to speak to you."

VOICE: "I have come a long way too."

MOTHER: "You know we are in London, and you like London, don't you?"

VOICE "Yes, I always liked London. Father, why do you look backward so much?"

MOTHER: "She wants you to look forward."

VOICE: "I was only twenty-five."

MOTHER: "That is right, dear. We are now beginning to understand more."

VOICE: "I did not suffer much. It was not too bad. This is wonderful, isn't it?"

FATHER: "So wonderful that we are still a bit amazed."

MOTHER: "You knew about the Reflectograph, so that shows you have been listening-in."

VOICE: "Of course I do. Learn all you can, Dad, but don't get tired. Uncle Jim is here, but I am holding the fort at the moment."

MOTHER: "You have to thank Red Cloud."

VOICE: "He told me when I came in to thank God. Can you hear me now, Dad? I am making a big effort."

MOTHER: "Do you know anything of the photograph we were speaking about this morning?"

VOICE: "The spirit photograph. Of course, Mother. Dad, be a good boy."

MOTHER: "Will we get a message from you tomorrow"

VOICE: "If I can work the thing."

MOTHER: "You get on the right side of the control; you will be all right. You are Scotch, you know."

VOICE: "Do not say, 'She was all we had in this world,' Dad. Say, 'She is all we have in the world.'"

MOTHER: "Good night, darling, see you tomorrow."

VOICE: "Good night, darling."

RED CLOUD: "It is the little things that count. You come seeking in truth. You come with the right idea. You come with the right soul."

M. B.: "Did she get on the right side of you, Red Cloud?"

RED CLOUD: "Red Cloud likes the young people. She is very pretty."

M. B.: "Oh, Red Cloud."

RED CLOUD: "You are thinking of faces. We are thinking of souls."

"Helen Macleod" was so evidential that I asked her father to write down this impression of the séance. Here it is:

HUGH MACLEOD'S STORY

Through the great kindness of Mrs. Estelle Roberts, my wife and I were privileged to attend a direct voice sitting held in her home.

About twenty people sat in the circle, wedged pretty closely together, so that no movement was possible without it being known to the others.

Red Cloud was not long in making his presence known. His voice appeared to proceed from the floor, though subsequent spirit voices spoke from mid-air and also from the ceiling.

Red Cloud addressed words of counsel to the sitters.

In a mighty voice he announced each spirit who desired to speak with a "Hold on!"

After one or two voices had greeted their friends, my wife and I were thrilled by a voice that at one time we thought was stilled for ever.

It said: "Mother, it is Helen speaking. It is Helen Macleod."

On replying, I was told that I wore her little watch on my wrist, and that her mother was wearing her ring. Her next piece of evidence was startling. She said to us, "I am coming with you to the Hand '—you know—the Reflectograph."

No one there present save our two selves knew of our projected visit to the Reflectograph.

She referred to her Uncle Jim as being present whilst she held the fort.

This was the only relative, apart from her parents, she had ever known. The fact of that name being given impressed me as being evidential.

On the day previous to this séance, we had had a sitting with Mrs. Roberts for the first time, our name being quite unknown to her.

Much of the evidence given on that occasion was amplified at the séance which has been described.

Our journey from Scotland was more than justified by the fresh hope given to us through this wonderful power of mediumship.

*   *   *

Helen was followed by a male voice calling for "Bertha."

The spirit recognised Mrs. Treloar when she spoke. Anyway, here is what was said. You will see how human it is.

The evidence is made up of trivialities—that is why it is evidence:

VOICE: "Bertha."

SITTER: "Yes."

VOICE: "It is George speaking."

SITTER: "My beloved, to be able to speak to you."

VOICE: "I am doing my best. Try to lift it up a little more."

MRS. TRELOAR: "He means the conditions. Lift them up. Say something funny."

(Sitters often get tense without realising it. This makes the conditions more difficult for the spirit voices.)

VOICE: "That sounds like Mrs. Treloar."

MRS. TRELOAR: "You seem to know me, but I do not know you."

SITTER: "Oh yes, you knew Mrs. Treloar, didn't you, George? (To Mrs. Treloar.) Don't you remember George Lawrence?"

MRS. TRELOAR: "Oh, yes, he was one of the stewards, wasn't he?"

(Mrs. Treloar is president of the Marylebone Spiritualist Association which holds services at the Queen's Hall on Sundays, at which George Lawrence may have been a steward.)

SITTER: "Now, George darling, I want to ask you a question. The last thing Jack said to me was, if I spoke to you or Sonny, to ask if you have a message for him."

VOICE: "Yes. Tell him I have been very close to him, and he is not to worry over what he is doing. Tell him I will see him through."

SITTER: "Thank you. You know what it means to all of us?"

VOICE: "Yes, I am going to see him through."

SITTER: "Will you give me something to take home to Joan?"

VOICE: "Give her my love. Listen, I am not satisfied with what S—** has done. There is no one here knows this. I am very sorry that he let the money go like that. It has left you rather badly off."

SITTER: "It has absolutely left me stranded, dear."

VOICE: "He has not looked after your interests. He promised you he would."

SITTER: "He has not looked after your interests. He promised you he would."

SITTER: "Yes, he did promise. They all broke their promises. You see I have not the means to carry on."

VOICE: "You will. I will see to that. Will you thank the medium for giving you this opportunity tonight?"

SITTER: "I have thanked her. I don't know what I would do without her. Do you remember what you used to call her?"

VOICE: "Little Angel. Be happy, dear."

SITTER: "I am trying to be, but the days are so long."

VOICE: "You tell them Spiritualism is a truth, but I wish the Spiritualists would be a little more human."

SITTER: "I have wished so, too."

VOICE: "I will come again."

SITTER: "Yes, I hope so."

MRS. TRELOAR: "Say good night for me, Mrs. Lawrence."

RED CLOUD: "She is not Mrs. Lawrence. She is Mrs. Scott."

** *Names and references suppressed by the author.*

Red Cloud always corrects mistakes, whether made by us, or if a voice is occasionally indistinct.

George Lawrence was followed by the piping voice of a little girl who gave her name, "Gwennie," and addressed her mother and aunt.

I am afraid they overwhelmed her with questions. There is an art in encouraging the spirit voices and making them feel confident and yet not "giving away" any evidence.

This little child was greeted with a succession of "What is your sister's name? Can you see us?" She could hardly speak.

She pleaded, "I am trying to talk," but she could not get past the barrage of questions.

A few other voices spoke, then Red Cloud brought the séance to an end.

As usual, his farewell was very impressive.

I quote two lines:

There is no love like the love that gives.
There is no service like the service that lives.

SIR ARTHUR CONAN DOYLE SPEAKS. SPIRIT NEWS OF COLONEL FAWCETT
[10th June, 1932]

THIS was one of the best sittings at which I have ever been present. Red Cloud told Lady Segrave she was going to be rewarded for her bravery. She had made public, a few weeks previously, the fact that she had proved her husband's survival. This, of course, had caused quite a sensation, and had proved rather a trial for her.

During the sitting, she felt something placed on her lap. When the lights went up she saw there, hot though the room was and stifling, a perfectly fresh red rose, still covered with moisture.

She was told it was a gift from her husband who afterwards spoke to her in a long, intimate conversation.

Mrs. Alice Liddell had a long conversation with her spirit doctor friend, who calls himself "B. G."

Since September, 1930, "B. G." has, at these voice séances, been giving her information concerning Colonel Fawcett, the missing explorer.

In order that you should understand the conversation between "B. G." and Mrs. Liddell, I must remind you of what is already known about the lost explorer.

Lieutenant-Colonel Fawcett, with his son Jack and a man named Raleigh Rimell, led an expedition into the heart of Brazil in 1925, with the object of discovering that great lost city of the South American continent, believed to have been one of the chief cradles of prehistoric civilisation.

He expected to be away for twenty months, and had arranged to send messages to the Daily News describing his adventures. He sent accounts to that newspaper, the first in May, 1925, and some more in December of the same year—and then there was silence. The expedition did not return.

Two years later, in 1927, a Brazilian engineer, named Robert Courteville, reported that he met Fawcett while he was motoring about 170 miles from the capital of Matto Grosso. Fawcett, he said, was shaking with fever, and his legs were terribly bitten by mosquitoes. He seemed to resent Courteville's interference, so they parted.

At that time, Courteville did not know the story of Fawcett's disappearance, but when he was told the facts, he said he would organise an expedition to bring him back to civilisation. This expedition apparently never materialised.

A man named Stephen Rattin thought he saw Fawcett in October of last year at Sao Paulo. Rattin described him as a white man with a long white beard and dressed in a costume of skins. He was being held prisoner by a tribe of Indians.

Rattin set out on an expedition, in the hope of finding Fawcett, but Mrs. Fawcett is not convinced that the man Rattin saw is her husband.

In September, 1930, Mrs. Liddell, when present at a voice séance, asked "B. G." whether he knew whom she was meeting the following Sunday.

"Yes," he replied, "the wife of an explorer, Mrs. Fawcett."

Mrs. Liddell then asked if Colonel Fawcett was in the buried city. She was told that he was, and that two of his party had passed on.

On 27th March, 1931, she went to another voice sitting, and "B. G." spoke to her again. He told her that Colonel Fawcett and his son Jack were still prisoners, and news of them might be obtained that year, but he could not be certain.

Now, let us return to the voice séance:

VOICE: "Good evening, everybody."

MRS. LIDDELL: "Good evening, B. G."

VOICE: "I have seen Fawcett. Let Mrs. Fawcett know. She has doubts. Tell her the boy is with another tribe. I have already told you that through "White Hawk" (the guide of another medium, Mrs. Barkel).

MRS. LIDDELL: "How is he?"

VOICE: "He is mentally ill."

MRS. LIDDELL: "Has he lost his memory?"

VOICE: "Not exactly, but the outside world is dim to him."

MRS. LIDDELL: "Have you heard how the rescue party is going on?

VOICE: "It is very difficult to make a pathway through the jungle."

MRS. LIDDELL: "I suppose the man Rattin will get through if anyone will."

VOICE: "He has found what he went for—the Golden City."

MRS. LIDDELL: "Will he remember it when he comes back?"

VOICE: "If he has complete rest. We will try and get him back alive in the body. Tell Mrs. Fawcett she will hear from Jack about six months afterwards."

MRS. LIDDELL: "After Colonel Fawcett is found? When will they get to him?"

VOICE: "It is difficult to say. One of the band has already

fallen out through swamp fever."

MRS. LIDDELL: "I do hope and pray he and Jack will get back."

VOICE: "You have a letter with you that Mrs. Fawcett wrote to you. Tell her from me that she must remember she will hardly recognise him at all."

MRS. LIDDELL: "I know, you told me before, that physically he was all right, but mentally not at all well."

VOICE: "What do you expect?"

Mrs. Liddell told me she had received a letter from Mrs. Fawcett only a few days before. It was in her bag, which she had taken to the séance unknown to anybody present.

Several other voices spoke to their friends present.

Then the evening was made still more dramatic. Red Cloud said there was a spirit who had asked permission to address us.

I am going to give you Hannen Swaffer's description of what occurred:

HANNEN SWAFFER'S DESCRIPTION

"You must watch and protect your mediums in the next two months."

It was the voice of Arthur Conan Doyle, speaking loudly to twenty people. The scene was the same séance-room in which Lady Doyle and her family heard Sir Arthur's voice at a previous sitting.

Doyle, vigorous, powerful, full of force, very earnest and very grave, came back and spoke of the great battle being waged between Spiritualism and the blundering forces that oppose everything that stands for progress.

Mrs. Constance Treloar, president of the Marylebone

Spiritualist Association, was present, in charge of the circle. Near her was George Craze, her immediate predecessor, and his wife.

Seated near me were Lady Carey and her great friend, Lady Hardinge. There were present, too, Maurice Barbanell, Dr. Rust, from Newport, Fifeshire. So was Lady Segrave.

The séance was a remarkable one. Lady Hardinge, a new-comer, got three spirit friends through, one after the other, all of them clear-cut entities, full of personality, who showered evidence upon her. The voice of the late Earl of St. Germans was particularly characteristic. She told me afterwards that the three people nearest to her in the other world had all come through.

Red Cloud, full of counsel, poured wisdom and inspiration upon the sitters. Dr. Rust, whom none of us knew by name, heard the highly-evidential voice of his wife, talking to him from Beyond. The evening was crammed with drama, yet holy as a sacrament.

Then towards the end of the sitting, Doyle came through.

"Doyle speaking," he said. "I asked permission just to come for a moment to offer congratulations on the new paper.—**"

"Go forward. Always stand for the truth. Fear no man. Do that which is good always. Do not worry over things. You have much to accomplish yet."

I thanked him for speaking to a home circle I know, and asked him to come along again.

"I will come again as often as I can," said Doyle. It is not so easy as it appears. Is Mr. Craze here? "Hearing Craze's voice, Doyle said, very dramatically, "Look after your medium."

It is because of the care exercised by the Marylebone Spiritualist Association in regard to Estelle Roberts, that

** *This was a reference to the Psychic News, a newspaper recently launched.*

she has developed so remarkably as an all-round medium.

"She is doing wonderful work," said Craze.

"Such wonderful work that you need to take care," replied the voice of Doyle.

Again came the warning: "You must watch and protect your mediums in the next two months.

"Listen to me, Swaffer. There is a great battle taking place, and you must watch our interests. You are able to forestall that which is being put into being. They will seek the best roses from your tree."

When Craze suggested that this was only the prelude to a greater fight, Doyle said, with an impressive forcefulness, "There is a great force opposing us, but we must go forward.

"Craze, they can never stem the tide. We are going to deluge the world. Truth is here at last."

Doyle, before going, sent to his wife "all my love and affection."

When I mentioned his son Denis, he replied, "God bless him and tell him to go forward in his work."

A SPIRIT'S STRANGE REQUEST
[24th June, 1932]

A VERY strange incident happened at this séance. Red Cloud told me there was a spirit present who wanted me to help him.

"Do I know him?" I asked.

"No," was the answer.

"Does he know me?" I enquired.

"No, but you can help him," Red Cloud replied.

In view of the message that came I have suppressed some of the names and the address he gave me. He spoke in an anxious and desperate voice:

VOICE: "I want to try and talk. I am George Vincent. I want someone to help my sister H—**. I was in the Merchant Service. I have been over here some years. Will someone help me?"

M. B.: Yes, I will help you. How can I get in touch with your sister?"

VOICE: "I want you to find Herbert L—**. He is at 38 G—** Road."

M. B. "What do you want me to say to him?"

VOICE: "Tell him to write to H—** before it is too late. Tell him that I gave the message. Tell him that we are anxious.

"It is six years now since it happened, and H—** is desperate. She is down by the sea. Do that for me, will you?"

M. B.: "Will he know where H—** is?"

VOICE "He will find her. What is today?"

M. B.: "Friday."

VOICE: "Then do it on Monday."

The address he gave was near my home. On the Monday I called there. It was a music shop. I hesitated before I walked in. After all, it was a little difficult to ask for a stranger and say, "I've come with a message from a spirit."

Still, in I walked. An assistant came forward.

"Do you know a Mr. Herbert L—**?" I asked.

"Yes," was the reply.

"May I speak to him?" I asked.

"He is not here at present," I was told. "He hires a studio here twice a week to give lessons."

I asked for his home address, but when I arrived there nobody was in. There was only one thing to do. I explained the whole circumstances in a letter, and included the message. I added my telephone number, and asked him to telephone me if he wanted any further information.

Two days later, a surprised Mr. L—** spoke to me on the telephone.

"Are you trying to convert me to Spiritualism?" he asked.

"No," I replied. "I am not interested in you to that extent. What I should like to know is, do you understand the message?"

"I refuse to tell you," he replied, and abruptly hung up his receiver.

** *Names and references suppressed by the author.*

FRENCH AND INDIAN NAMES
[8th July, 1932]

THE séance that night was perfect. The voices were strong and clear. An Indian woman present had a long conversation with her niece.

"Auntie," the voice said, "it is —**. Do not worry over uncle's affairs. Tell him I am helping. There will be no case going into court. Do you understand?"

SITTER: "Oh, yes, I do."

VOICE: "I want to help you. You have travelled so far to hear me. I tried so hard to get through. —**'s aeroplane crashed."

SITTER: "But the aeroplane was not found."

VOICE: "It was in the sea."

SITTER: "How very sad."

VOICE: "Don't tell his mother. She thinks he will be found. He has come back so many times, but now he is dead."

SITTER: "Quite true."

VOICE: "God bless you, darling."

SITTER "God bless you."

VOICE: "I try to watch over you all I can."

After this voice had spoken, there followed one of those flashes of spontaneous wit, so typical of Red Cloud.

It is necessary to explain that Red Cloud gives us all names—Mrs. Treloar has become Rachel, while I am called John.

Red Cloud said: "They are good souls here tonight."

** *Names and references suppressed by the author.*

M. B. (jokingly): "Only good ones come here, Red Cloud."

MRS. TRELOAR: "Except those who come to be helped."

M. B.: "I will pray for you, Rachel."

RED CLOUD: "John! Charity begins at home."

If I attempted to record all the voices at each of these séances, this book would become a tome.

I am compelled, therefore, to make a selection. The dialogue that follows is particularly interesting, as the French names were heard most distinctly:

VOICE: "Mother! Paddy here; it is Paddy, mother. Father is here."

SITTER: "Are you both together?"

VOICE: "Just keep calm. We have Madame de Beury here with us. She asked me to ask you to convey her love to Richet and Miss Hett. Mother, this is wonderful."

SITTER: "Yes, it is."

VOICE: "Do not worry about it."

SITTER: "No, I will not worry, but I hoped you would come."

VOICE: "I am trying so hard. Can you hear me?"

SITTER: "Quite well."

VOICE: "Mother, it was a big shock to you when Father passed over, but he came for me, Mother. We are helping Lopez. He needs all our help."

SITTER: "Yes."

VOICE: "I am so glad to hear you."

SITTER: "I can hear you very well."

VOICE: "I am trying so hard to talk to you. It is not an easy task they have set me, but I would do anything in the world to get to you."

SITTER: "Yes, I hoped you would come."

VOICE: "Are you happy?"

SITTER: "Yes, darling; are you?"

VOICE: "Ever so, because we know you understand. Mother, you will not forget to convey Madame de Beury's love to Richet and Miss Hett?"

SITTER: "All my love to her and you."

VOICE: "I come very close to you and try to help you."

SITTER: "Thank you so much."

VOICE: "Goodbye, darling, I will come back again."

SITTER: "Yes, I will come again."

VOICE: "Thank God! Thank God!"

Red Cloud immediately followed and said to the sitter:

"Do you know someone Hussey Frankau? Your boy wanted me to tell you he saw him the other day."

Red Cloud often adds another scrap of evidence when the voice has gone.

EDGAR WALLACE RETURNS
[23rd September, 1932]

ON this night we had a remarkable séance. There had been no sittings for several weeks—Estelle Roberts had a much-needed rest during August.

It is necessary to explain that early in September the Psychic News published a series of automatic writings, said to have been given by Edgar Wallace through a medium, describing his life after death.

This script was attacked by Bob Curtis, Wallace's former secretary, in the Sunday Dispatch.

Among those who spoke this night was Edgar Wallace.

This is Swaffer's description of the séance:

HANNEN SWAFFER'S DESCRIPTION

"I gave you that script. I sat for my photograph. This is Wallace here speaking, whether you like it or not. . . It is damnably hard to be disbelieved when you are trying your utmost to make them understand. . .

"There were comments about an Indian, and there will be more comments because I have come through again. . . Whether the world likes it or not, I am going to come through. They can laugh and they can scoff, but I am coming back. . . I will break down every barrier."

These are some of the statements made by Edgar Wallace.

The voice circle was crowded with drama, packed with incident. Evidence poured through for two hours. There was nothing hesitant. Names, facts and proofs poured through from the spirit world.

Before the circle started, Mrs. Constance Treloar, as usual, warned all the sitters, of whom there were more than a score, not to volunteer one fact, or guess at a name, but to wait for the spirit voices to prove their identities for themselves. The rule was rigidly obeyed.

I call as a witness of what happened Edward Ayearst Reeves, F.R.A.S., F.R.G.S., not a credulous person, but a man of scientific attainment, one who in 1916 was President of the Geographical Section of the British Association.

"It was astonishing," he said afterwards. "The evidence was wonderful."

Now, before Wallace came through, Mr. Reeves, who has been investigating Spiritualism for some time, and who has kept a careful record of all his evidence, had direct voice messages from Claude Alexander, his brother David, Harold Watkins, the explorer who was drowned off Greenland, his wife's nephew, Jim Waters and his own son.

Alexander chaffed him for being there, in a humorous, keenly intelligent voice. "I am glad to see you," he said, "but I didn't expect to see you here—with your scientific mind."

"But, you know, Claude, I have been interested for some time," said Reeves.

Then, after his brother David had spoken to Mr. Reeves— and a son who passed over as long ago as 1885 —we heard the voice, through the trumpet, of Harold Watkins.

"Oh! really, my dear boy," said Reeves, who is the map curator and instructor in practical astronomy and surveyor to the Royal Geographical Society, and whose pupil Watkins was, as were half the members of his party of explorers.

"Mr. Reeves, you remember me?" asked the voice.

"Of course," said Reeves.

"I have not been here long," came the voice through the trumpet. "I was drowned. I was among the Eskimos. I have found my mother. I should particularly like Margaret to know."

"I have written to her," said Reeves, who knew that Margaret was Harold Watkins's fiancée.

"I am alive, not dead, not dead," said the voice, the repeated words being uttered very loudly the second time.

"Segrave told me. . . He helped me to come," went on the voice.

"Thank you for what you have said to me," said Reeves.

"Tell Sir William that I have been back," replied the spirit voice. "Tell them all about it. . . I went under the ice. . . I have been trying to get at you, in the Society."

The "Sir William" referred to, Reeves told me after the sitting, was Admiral Sir William Goodenough, President of the Royal Geographical Society, who took a great interest in Watkins and his trip.

Then we heard Red Cloud, the guide, speaking.

"It is the young explorer," he said.

"It is very good of you to allow him to come along," replied Reeves.

"It is the law of attraction," explained Red Cloud.

"You knew him, and he belonged to your Geographical Society."

"Yes, he worked in a room I lent him," said Reeves. "Thank you, Red Cloud."

"Don't thank me," said Red Cloud, as usual. "Thank God."

"I do thank God for using you," said Reeves.

Although I am using a copy of verbatim notes taken down

in a cabinet by the stenographer, the real witness of all this is Mr. Reeves himself, who was only too willing to bear tribute to the naturalness of all the conversation of his spirit friends and the evidence they gave of their identity.

Then there was another most dramatic scene. My witness is Mrs. Williams of the Mead, Wallington.

On 1st August, knowing nothing about our case, she wrote to the Earl of Cottenham, after having seen one of his articles in the Daily Express, and asked him for the address of a medium.

In consequence, she had a trance sitting with Mrs. Roberts, but told her nothing. At that sitting, Red Cloud invited her to a direct-voice séance. So she was there.

Suddenly we heard a voice.

"I want to talk to Daisy," it said.

"Good evening," said Mrs. Williams, whose name is Daisy.

"This is Pearl George Black, of the Canadian Army," went on the voice. "Unfortunately, I committed suicide. I am quite close to you, my dear. How can I thank you for all you have done for me? You have been my light and inspiration... You people here tonight, don't ever let fear get you, like it did me."

"It did get him badly," said Mrs. Williams, who disclosed her identity when the sitting was over, and who added that, when a nurse during the war, she met Pearl Black in a train, and became a close friend.

"I was a doctor, too," went on the voice. "Daisy, I tried to show myself. You know what you used to call me— "The Black Pearl."

"Yes, that is right," said Mrs. Williams.

"Daisy dear, I do thank you for lifting me up," went on the spirit. "I was in utter darkness and you brought me to light."

"Keep on rising, Pearl," said his woman friend.

"A good many of us would rise if we had friends like you," went on the voice.

Then there followed an intimate conversation, which I will not repeat, but full of proof that the voice knew all about his friend's present circumstances.

"Some Indian pushed me here," went on the voice, explaining how he had come to the circle. "I would go to the end of the world to find Daisy. She was the one friend I had. . . I was just full of fear of life. It got me in the end. I shot myself. God help me!"

"Never mind, Pearl," said Mrs. Williams. "You will come through."

"I am getting on," replied the voice. "If I can stick by you, I will stick to the end. I was a stranger and you helped me. God bless you, Daisy."

"Thank you, Red Cloud," said Mrs. Williams, when her spirit friend had gone.

"Even as you do unto one of these, you do it unto the Father," replied Red Cloud. "To help one soul out of darkness is to do something for your God."

Then we had a volunteered statement from Mrs. Williams.

"It is splendid," she said. "I am a stranger to everyone here. Nobody knows anything about my friend Pearl."

Later, she added that one evening she felt him come into her room and kiss her. She turned to her daughter and said: "Pearl is dead." At that moment he had shot himself.

Then a British Major who has been conducting scientific research at Riga, had a most interesting conversation with his friend Stuart Johnston, a subaltern, who was killed in the war.

Although I have not got a note of what he said, the spirit voice carried on for five minutes or more a most animated conversation.

He asked, "Is Esme here?" That was the name of the Major's wife, who was, unfortunately, unable at the last moment to be present.

He volunteered names—Beatrice, Michael, who was a Russian friend, Tress, Molly, Cecil, Hamish, Oliver and Dobbie. He talked about Riga where he had been trying to get through to his friend the Major.

All these names were volunteered by the Stuart Johnston voice.

Commenting upon them Red Cloud said, "I got them out of the medium's book," this being said, of course, with a laugh.

Afterwards I learned that, in the Major's own circle at Riga, apports had been received, and that on one occasion Professor Blacker, president of the Riga Psychical Research Society, more or less a sceptic, marked in the garden a flower, and then, in the séance room, asked the spirits if they could bring it in.

Shortly afterwards, the marked flower arrived, and when they went back to the garden, they found that its stem fitted the broken stalk of the plant.

Another of the sitters was a woman, whose name I did not get, who spoke to a friend who had been drowned abroad. His concern was that some of the family thought he had committed suicide. He assured this woman friend that he had been bathing.

"Yes, I believe it, my dear," she said. "I never thought you had committed suicide. Don't worry about some of the others."

This spirit was most concerned, though, about his friends' fears about his passing, and he implored the woman to reassure his family.

This she promised to do.

The Edgar Wallace voice was heard right at the end of the sitting.

I knew that Wallace would turn up, because I had been told so at my home circle on the previous Sunday. On two occasions, before, Wallace had tried to get through at the Estelle Roberts circle, but, with his extraordinary vigour and over-enthusiasm, he tried to do so before he had mastered the conditions of communication.

Well, Wallace did get through, and for ten minutes carried on a conversation with me, continually emphasizing the fact that the Wallace script which had been published in the Psychic News was genuine, that the spirit photograph taken by John Myers was genuine, and adding, "Tell—** not to be a fool."

Now, it did not sound like Edgar's voice. My experience of the direct voice is that the earth voice becomes more easily recognised as the communicator becomes more used to speaking.

But, certainly, all Wallace's personality was there —all his dominant insistence. There was not one word in a long conversation out of keeping with Wallace's own personality, which I knew so well.

Afterwards, Red Cloud said, "Wallace does not know his own strength. Mind, he is a good soul. He has a good personality. But he does not know his own power. Just at the moment it is a little unsafe for him to use my medium more than he has done tonight. But he will come through again.

"The next time he talks to you he will have something important to tell."

Afterwards, when Sir Henry Segrave spoke, as he invariably does when Lady Segrave is present, he remarked to me that he had been doing his best to instruct Wallace how to master the means by which his voice came through.

"He certainly does push," he said, laughing.

"It took four of us to hold Wallace down."

Segrave's personality grows at every sitting. You get evidence, more and more, of his charming and gracious personality, his alertness of mind, and the clearness of his intelligence.

He spoke to his wife of their wedding anniversary, which was approaching.

"I live for these talks, Boy," she said.

I know of my own knowledge the difference these circles have made to her life.

Over a score of spirit voices was heard, all of them proving themselves to the sitters.

It was a wonderful evening. People who have not attended one of these séances may mock and jeer. They may say whatever they like. But, all over the world, they are bringing comfort to thousands of people every week.

*** Names and references suppressed by the author.*

SIR ERNEST SHACKLETON SPEAKS
[21st October, 1932]

THERE was a dramatic incident at this séance. One of the voices said, "Sir Ernest Shackleton speaking, I want my wife."

A woman had been brought into the circle by a Miss Thomas as her friend. Following the usual custom, she was not introduced to anybody and her name was not given. I learnt afterwards that she had had a private sitting with Mrs. Estelle Roberts, but even then her name was not disclosed.

When the voice announced itself, I asked whether anyone knew him. The lady next to me answered. She was Lady Shackleton.

"I am a little deaf, I am afraid," she said. "Can you give me a message?"

I repeated to Lady Shackleton word for word the messages that came through the trumpet.

VOICE (to other sitters): "I want to tell my dear one that her sister is here with me tonight."

LADY SHACKLETON: "How wonderful."

VOICE: "We are all together here. I am awfully sorry I am not quite proficient at this. I will come back again."

LADY SHACKLETON: "Can you give me a message?"

VOICE: "How are the boys?"

LADY SHACKLETON: "Well, I hope the other one is all right."

VOICE: "Yes, there is one abroad."

LADY SHACKLETON: "Can you help him?"

VOICE: "I have helped him. I come down to the Palace to fetch you."

LADY SHACKLETON: "I am always listening for the sound of your voice."

VOICE: "I was so anxious you should not fail to come along."

LADY SHACKLETON: "I would have come if I had to come on all fours."

VOICE: "You never did fail me, never, never, NEVER. Darling, I am so happy that you are staying now at the Palace. You see you are not very far away from this medium then, and I feel somehow it is a close link for me. I will endeavour to speak to you again."

LADY SHACKLETON: "Are you happy?"

VOICE: "I am waiting for you, dear, waiting for you."

LADY SHACKLETON: "Very busy, aren't you, doing all kinds of things?"

VOICE: "I am still endeavouring to do those things which will be of help to humanity. God bless you, my darling. Try and come again some day because your dear sister wants to speak to you."

RED CLOUD: "You know that is one of God's gentlemen."

LADY SHACKLETON: "Thank you, Red Cloud."

RED CLOUD: "Greater love hath no man than this to lay down his life for his friend."

I asked Lady Shackleton whether the messages were evidential. He had given her a message regarding some relatives and he had also referred to the address where she lived.

These were evidential, she said, although, of course, she could not be certain that it was her husband.

I told her that for a first attempt it was fairly successful, and that at later sittings his voice would become stronger.

A female voice carried on a long conversation with her brother, who afterwards told me he had come from Johannesburg, where his sister had spoken to him at another direct-voice séance.

VOICE: "Arthur, I want Arthur. Arthur dear, it is Margaret."

SITTER: "I am so pleased to see you. I was hoping you would come."

VOICE: "Why did you not bring Harold tonight?"

SITTER: "I don't think he would like to come just yet. I have not spoken to him about it very much."

VOICE: "And Barbara?"

(You will notice it is the spirit voice which gives the names.)

SITTER: "I will go and see her next Monday and tell her then."

VOICE: "Daddy is here."

SITTER: "Give him my love, darling. You know, when I go back, I am going to sit in the same place as before."

VOICE: "I will speak to you again."

SITTER: "I could not hear you so well the last time I spoke to you."

VOICE: "That was out in South Africa."

SITTER: "Yes, quite right."

VOICE: "You see the mediums here are so much more trained."

SITTER: "Yes, I know, darling."

Red Cloud's comment on this was, "She was about twenty, wasn't she, and had what you call consumption?"

"Yes," said the sitter, "that is right."

"She has not got it now," Red Cloud told him. "She is very

happy to talk to you."

"This is James Gow speaking," said the next voice.

SITTER: "But I never knew you. You are a grandfather of mine."

VOICE: "Of course I am, that is why I have come."

SITTER: "Well, this is very evidential."

VOICE: "I have come to help you in your distressed state. You must not be worried in any way."

SITTER: "It is very difficult for me, you know."

VOICE: "But I want you not to worry. There are several of us helping you. Do you remember Parker?"

SITTER: "Another grandfather of mine."

VOICE: "We are going to put matters right."

SITTER: "I do not know what to do for the best."

VOICE: "Do not do anything, but wait for us to do things for you."

SITTER: "But how shall I know?"

VOICE: "We shall make ourselves quite clear on that at the right time."

A childish girl's voice, which gave her age as four, spoke to her mother. She brought her own evidence. She referred to her toys and she described in detail the frieze in her nursery and the animals embroidered on her frock. The child reminded them of her birthday which was due shortly, and promised to be present at the party which they were giving in her honour.

A SPIRIT THANKS LADY SEGRAVE
[4th November, 1932]

AMID the mass of evidence that night I have selected the remarkable communication that Lady Segrave received.

Red Cloud had told her that there was a boy who wished to speak to her. He wanted to thank her for something she had done.

He was immediately followed by the voice of a young man who said:

"I want to offer my thanks to Lady Segrave. I am Patrick G—**."

He gave his full name, but it cannot be disclosed at present.

"I want to thank you for the help you have given my mother," he continued. "Will you please give her a message? Thank her for the flowers she put on my grave."

Lady Segrave promised to give this message to his mother.

"Thank her for what she did for the chauffeur," the boy went on. "He took her to my grave."

The chauffeur's name was given. It was a French name and it was spelt by the voice.

Then Red Cloud followed.

"Did you understand the boy's message?" he asked Lady Segrave. "If not I will repeat it."

Slowly and deliberately Red Cloud said

"He says his mother went to Paris and she went with the taxi-man to the boy's grave. The boy wants you to thank her for what she gave to G—**, the taxi man, who, he says, WAS

THE LAST PERSON TO SEE HIM ALIVE."

"You know, little lady," he continued, "that boy did not commit suicide. What happened was this. He went into what the French people call a café and drank veronal to make him sleep. He drank too much. His motive was not suicide but sleep.

"That is what your world fails to understand. It is the motive that counts."

It was very impressive. A human drama was being played in the darkness of the séance-room.

The message was passed on by Lady Segrave to the boy's mother, a woman whom she had met quite casually a year ago.

The mother confirmed that it was a remarkable piece of evidence. All the boy said was true. The name of the French chauffeur was correctly given. It was a great comfort to her to know that her boy did not commit suicide.

Now, as often happens, the names have had to be suppressed. The mother does not wish her identity to be disclosed. For the same reason, the boy's name and the chauffeur's are not given.

Young Patrick G—** was followed by a voice that announced itself:

"Hullo, it is Jack Hall speaking."

Then in the dark I listened to this thrilling love episode:

SITTER: "God bless you, darling. Come quite close to me."

VOICE: "Can you hear me? Don't cry, dear."

SITTER: "Have you a message for Kathleen?"

VOICE: "Give my little girl all my love, dear."

SITTER: "How are they getting on? How is Douglas?"

VOICE: "He will be coming home quite soon."

SITTER: "What was the anniversary yesterday?"

VOICE: "My birthday."

(When the sitter heard this reply she was rather disappointed.)

"No, darling," she burst out.

But the voice insisted, "It is. I am not going to say death."

"Oh yes," replied the sitter, "it is a real birthday, isn't it? Do you hear me when I speak to you after my prayers in the morning?"

VOICE: "I hear every word you say. I always do. God bless you, Rene. Give my love to Phyllis. Look after the boys."

SITTER: "Look after them, dear."

VOICE: "I love you all so much."

(Here the sound of kisses was heard through the trumpet.)

SITTER: "God bless you, my love."

VOICE: "Come back some other time."

SITTER: "I am coming again to have a quiet chat with Red Cloud and you."

VOICE: "Yes. In April. Our wedding day."

** *Names and references suppressed by the author.*

DENNIS NEILSON-TERRY SPEAKS
[3rd December, 1932]

RED CLOUD was in a very jocular mood. Again and again during the evening he said, "Do not say, Is that you, Tom?"

This was a reference to the warning that Mrs. Treloar gives at every séance. She tells all the sitters not to give any facts away.

"Do not say, Is that you, Tom, Dick or Harry?" she says, "but let the spirit voices prove their own identity."

She has said this so often that we always laugh when she repeats it, although, of course, it is a necessary warning to the newcomers.

Red Cloud fastened on to it almost at the beginning of this séance.

"There is a stranger here," he said. "Don't say, Is that you, Tom?" Of course we all laughed.

One of the first "voices" to speak was one which announced itself:

"Hullo, Father, Jack Doyle."

He was immediately greeted by his father: "That is my boy. Come along, Jack."

VOICE: "How are you, Father?"

SITTER: "All right. Is Mother there?"

VOICE: "She is going to try to speak. I have only just come, Father, to make room for Mother."

SITTER: "Are you going on all right?"

VOICE: "Hold the fort. I am going to send Mother in."

He was immediately followed by a woman's voice which said: "It is Edie speaking."

There was a long conversation between Edie and her husband. I have given this in detail, word for word as it was spoken.

SITTER: "Hullo, dear."

VOICE: "Jack pushed me through. We are together here."

SITTER: "I know you are, dear."

VOICE: "I am very happy to come."

SITTER: "Fine, isn't it?"

VOICE: "How are the two children"

SITTER: "They are all right now."

VOICE: "One has had scarlet fever, hasn't she?"

SITTER: "Quite right. She is all right again now."

VOICE: "Have you had the path done?"

This question caused the husband great surprise. He was astonished that his wife should be familiar with details happening around him as trivial as this, but, after all, trivialities though they are, they are very evidential.

SITTER: "DO YOU KNOW ABOUT THAT? I didn't want it done, but the County Council made me do it."

VOICE: "Yes, I know."

SITTER: "And they have put me to a lot of expense."

VOICE: "Yes, I know. I am so sorry for you. I love you so much, dear. I am waiting for you."

"You won't have to wait much longer," was the sitter's reply, in a voice firm with the knowledge that life goes on.

SITTER: "Can you see me now?"

VOICE: Yes. You have got my tie-pin on."

SITTER "That is right, dear."

VOICE: "It was my ring."

SITTER: "Quite right, it was."

VOICE: "I am so glad to come."

SITTER: "It is capital for a first effort. Has Red Cloud been giving you some lessons?"

VOICE: "No."

SITTER: "Jolly good for a first start."

VOICE: "Some keep much more calm than others."

(Often when spirit voices come for the first time they are so excited that they lose control of the "power" necessary to speak through the trumpet.)

SITTER: "I am so glad to talk to you, you know, dear."

(The reply to this was the sound of kisses coming through the trumpet.)

VOICE: "Be happy, dear. Don't do too much walking."

SITTER: "It keeps me healthy."

VOICE: "I have seen you with the case."

SITTER: "Oh, yes, with the little case."

VOICE: "God bless you, dear."

Red Cloud immediately followed and said to this man, "That was your wife and your son."

"Yes, thank you, Red Cloud," he answered. Red Cloud as usual said, "Thank God."

The next voice to speak was the voice of another Indian guide, who spoke to one of the sitters present. This guide gave him a great deal of information concerning his wife's health, and some advice about her mediumship.

He was followed by a voice giving the name of Sir Vincent Caillard which spoke to one of the ladies present. She was Lady Caillard, who had recently published a book describing her conversations with him elsewhere.

Sir Vincent called her by her nickname "Birdie."

"Can you hear me?" he asked "I am happy to come and talk to you."

LADY CAILLARD: "I have brought you some roses."

VOICE: "They are not red ones."

LADY CAILLARD: "No, I know. I could not get them."

VOICE: "Never mind. Can you hear me quite well?"

LADY CAILLARD: "Yes, darling."

VOICE: "I will come again soon."

LADY CAILLARD: "I know you are shy about talking in front of people."

VOICE: "God bless you for publishing the book."

LADY CAILLARD: "I know you are pleased."

VOICE: "It helps the world so much when you set out to give the truth."

LADY CAILLARD: "I am so glad."

There were some other references to private matters which I have deliberately omitted.

Lady Caillard told me it was all very convincingly characteristic, and it was certainly her husband.

Red Cloud's comment on Sir Vincent was, "He is a very nice white man."

"Yes," said Hannen Swaffer, "he was a nice man. I remember him on the earth."

"He Is," replied Red Cloud. "We are not 'wassers', we are 'issers'. Hold on!"

Then we heard:

"This is Dr. Stewart speaking. Where is Mrs. Williams?"

"I am Mrs. Williams," replied a voice in the circle.

VOICE: "I want to come and talk to you for a few minutes if I can."

MRS. WILLIAMS: "I do not quite remember you. I know

so many doctors. Is my mother with you?"

VOICE: "Yes, she is here."

MRS. WILLIAMS: "How is she?"

VOICE: "You do not remember me very well."

MRS. WILLIAMS: "No, I was not at home much."

VOICE: "I believe you have got me muddled up with someone else. I am Stewart, the Scottish doctor."

MRS. WILLIAMS: "Oh yes! I know you quite well."

VOICE: "I would have been very disappointed if I had gone away without your knowing me. I helped you."

MRS. WILLIAMS: "You started me on my work first, and I am still doing the same kind. Have you joined up with —**?"

She was interrupted by the voice which said, "Pearl, yes, a very wonderful spirit."

(Pearl had already spoken to her, as I have recorded, at a previous voice sitting.)

MRS. WILLIAMS: "He helped me with a case six weeks ago."

VOICE: "It was a lady."

MRS. WILLIAMS: "Yes, I never nurse gentlemen."

When he had gone, Mrs. Williams volunteered the information that, "The doctor started me off on the work that I do now. No one knew about it. It was thirty-five years ago."

Red Cloud told us the "power" was getting very weak. He explained that the medium had had a shock during the week, which made it a little difficult for him to get the voices through as clearly as usual.

The voice which followed him was not very strong, but it called for "Mary." The response came from Mary Glynne, the actress, who was present.

"It is Dennis," went on the "voice." (It was Dennis

** *Names and references suppressed by the author.*

Neilson-Terry, her husband.)

"Who is with you?" he asked. "I have got to get accustomed to this. Can you hear me?"

"Yes," replied Mary Glynne.

Then, Dennis Terry spoke to his sister Phyllis Neilson-Terry, who was also present:

"Thank you for what you are doing for Mary."

"What is that, darling?" she replied.

"Looking after her," was his answer.

He insisted that Miss Neilson-Terry had been very kind to his wife. He also gave them some advice about the health of his parents, and sent a message to one of his friends.

"This is terribly difficult," he said, "but I shall do it better next time."

The last voice to speak was that of Sir Henry Segrave, who has now a perfect mastery of the trumpet. He conversed in whispers with Lady Segrave, and it was done so well that the rest of the circle could hardly hear what he said.

THE SPIRITS' "MERRY XMAS"
[16th December, 1932]

BECAUSE it was Christmas, several children spoke to their parents and friends. "It is getting near Christmas," said Jackie, now a regular visitor to the circle, speaking with his usual boyish exuberance.

"Yes, my darling," said his foster-mother, "a week today. What are you going to do then?"

"Come with you," said Jackie. Then he went on with one of his long talks with her.

He was followed by a small piping voice who asked for "Daddy, Daddy."

"Is your daddy here?" enquired Mrs. Constance Treloar. "What is your name?"

"Peter," was the answer. "Daddy, Daddy," went on his baby voice. "It is Peter, Peterkin."

Peter, I learnt afterwards, passed on when he was only sixteen months old, but had grown up, of course, in the spirit world. Yet he returned to bring a Christmas greeting to his parents.

"Mummy, I'm so happy," he said. "Is John here?" "No," said his father, "but I will take a message to him."

"Kiss him and Wendy," came Peterkin's voice.

The sound of kisses was heard coming through the trumpet.

"I have come with my grandfather John," Peter told them. "He is pushing me. Gladys has helped too," he volunteered.

There was a long conversation between them.

"What about my rocking horse up in the top room?" piped Peter.

"Yes," said his father, "that is still there and I ride it sometimes."

"Funny Daddy," said Peter.

Then he said, "I am not in pain now. Do not grieve for Peter."

"No, darling," they told him.

"Daddy, Daddy," he shouted excitedly, "there is a nice doctor here. He said I died of meningitis."

"Quite right," said the father. "You did not have much pain, did you, sweetheart?"

"But I did not die," Peter insisted. "I am only having a joke with you," said his father.

"What have we got in the house now which runs about?" they asked him.

"A dog," shouted Peter. "Give my love to Dodo."

Then he told them how he plays with his sister Wendy, and asked them to give his love to Nettie and Johnnie.

"I like the little dog," he said, "but you did not have her when I was here. You have somebody now to take my place."

"Nobody takes your place, Peterkin," he was told.

"I do not mind," he answered. "Good night, Mummy; good night, Daddy."

Then came another child's voice.

"I am Daphne," she said.

"Yes," said a sitter.

"Mummy," went on the voice, "there are such a lot of people here. Is John here? John has been playing with the barrow. Daphne plays with the barrow too."

The child was apparently embarrassed by seeing the score of sitters in the circle, strangers to her.

"Tell them not to listen to Daphne," she said. "This is Daphne Williams talking."

Then, when her mother asked her who brought her she replied, "Daddy's uncle." But she did not know which one. She added all she knew was that a guide said, "Go into the box, Daphne, and you can talk."

So Daphne went into the box.

Then two elderly sitters got a woman friend who always visits them when they sit.

"Annie," said a voice, "Annie Mason." Then she called for "Sarah."

"Have you got my thimble, Sarah?" she asked. "Yes, in my bag," was the reply.

"I often come and sit in my own chair by the fire," she told them.

She spoke of her shawl and her cushion which they had put on it in memory of her.

There was a long and intimate conversation all about Christmas, and how she would join in the festivities. Then came Bobby.

"I am your brother, dear," he said to his sister. He spoke of a little lady he had brought with him, one known to the sitter, a woman who wanted him to say, "She is very happy over what you did a little while ago for her husband."

"I am helping you down at the hotel," volunteered Bobby. "I like the little dog you have got with you. Has Mother got over my passing?"

There were lots of details like this.

"Tell my sister," went on Bobby, "she is getting closer to

the truth."

"Which one do you mean?" asked the sitter.

"The eldest one," said Bobby.

Mrs. Morrel, a medium who was present, had a long talk with her coloured guide Lulu, who spoke to all the sitters she knew in the circle. She had met them at different sittings with her medium. They told me they recognised Lulu's voice, her characteristics and her personality generally.

Among the spirit visitors who came, was the wife of C. B. Parrish, a man I knew some years ago. The name of "Hettie" was called. It was his wife who had passed on, suffering from the terrible agonies of cancer.

"Mr. Swaffer is here, dear," said the voice, recognising Hannen Swaffer, to whom she had spoken through another medium in his own home circle years ago.

She spoke of her son John, and revealed a knowledge of all that was happening around her husband.

It was the largest voice circle we had held. There were present twenty-six people, and eighteen spirit voices addressed us during the night.

THE NEW YEAR'S MESSAGE
[30th December, 1932]

A PATHETIC child's voice, "Daddy, it is Micky. It is Micky speaking."

This was one of the outstanding voices that spoke to us. For over an hour and a half the voices of the "dead" addressed their friends.

It was a night full of evidence.

Each voice spoke clearly and distinctly. Little Micky had returned to comfort his father. He wanted his mother to know he had been back, because "she was so ill."

"Have you seen Mummy?"asked his father.

"Yes. I have been to see her," replied the voice, "Granny took me."

"How is Mother?" his father enquired.

"She is a little better," his spirit son told him. "She is worrying."

"What is she worrying about?" he was asked. Because I died," said Micky. "One, two, three of us are all here now. Poor Mummy."

It was a pathetic incident.

"Daddy, tell Mummy Micky always loves her. I wish she would not be so sad, Daddy."

"When are we going to sit again, dear?" said his father, wondering when his home circle would recommence.

"Not for a long while, because Mummy must get strong. Mummy had another little Micky, but he died. Don't be unhappy. We are all together. I love you all the time."

And so another parent was given solace in the hour of need. Yes, "Comfort the mourner," said the Great Teacher, two thousand years ago, and a little child was fulfilling the message.

"Mother, Pat speaking. It is Pat," said the first voice that spoke that night.

"Yes," came the reply from a lady in the circle.

"Mother," insisted the voice, "it is Pat speaking. Don't you know your own son? I have come with Father," he told her.

The spirit recognised another friend of his who was present.

"Hullo, Piccy," he said. "So nice of you to come and talk to me. You will have a surprise presently."

He thanked "Piccy" for being so good to his mother. Before he left, he gave his full name. "Pat Harrison speaking," he told them.

Red Cloud added another bit of evidence:

"He brought his father with him. His father was murdered."

"Yes, that is quite right," said the sitter.

"He was stabbed in the back," said Red Cloud, "and the wife has prayed for the murderer. That is a lesson to you all. Do good to those who hate you."

Pat Harrison was followed by a voice giving its name as "Cousin Edwin speaking." He wanted the man who had been addressed as "Piccy," and called him by his Christian name, "Cecil." Edwin told him, "Alice is here, your sister, and your father too. I am going out so that your father can speak."

Before the father spoke Red Cloud again interposed:

"Is your father William Robert, or Robert William?"

"Robert William," was the reply.

"Well," said Red Cloud, "he gave it as William Robert, but your mother said it was the wrong way about."

The father immediately spoke.

"William, my son, where are you?" he said.

He asked his son to give his love to Ernest, William and Bob.

He showed an intimate knowledge of all that was happening around his son, and gave him some advice concerning a matter that was causing some difficulty.

"William Jolly speaking," announced the next voice. "God bless you, my boy."

"This is a treat," said the sitter who was being addressed.

"Your mother is here, my boy." Her name was given.

The spirit father told his son that he knew all about his worries.

"I want you to understand," he said, "that I know the two states of mind you are in." He promised to guide him, and help him.

They spoke for a while, yes, the living and the dead, as naturally as any father and son ever speak on earth.

"I want you to help the next one," said Red Cloud. "He is a stranger here. Hold on!"

"Bernard speaking," immediately came the voice. "Ed," he called. Bernard immediately claimed his father, mother and two brothers who were present.

"I am so excited," he said. "Dad, I am not dead. It is good to hear you."

"Are you happy, my son?" asked his father.

"How can I be happy without you all?" was the reply. Do you believe it now?" he asked his brother.

"I am trying so hard to believe," was the rather strange

reply.

The rest of the circle laughed. The idea of someone trying to believe in his brother's survival, while he was talking to him, seemed somewhat funny.

"How are the love birds?" enquired Bernard.

When he was asked by his mother what his work was in the Other World, he replied, "Looking after you, darling."

"You had plenty of pluck when I was killed," he told her.

Referring to his death, he told his parents, "It was not all his fault. It was a blind corner."

"How is the girl, Len?" he asked his other brother. "When are you going to name the day?

"Pretty soon," was the reply.

"I will be there," the spirit voice told him.

He spoke to them about their own home circle, and gave some advice about the development of their mediumship. He promised to arrange some healing for his father.

"Don't sit down and think of me as a blooming spook," he said, "because I am not."

Just as he left he shouted his name, "Bernard Heath."

Red Cloud added another piece of evidence. "He was killed on a motor-bike," he told them.

"Fred Roberts speaking," announced the next voice. I have called my name three times—can you not hear me? It is the first time I have spoken like this."

"It is so nice of you to come," said the sitter to whom he spoke.

"Have you brought anyone with you?" she asked him.

"Shall I tell you whom? Bob," Fred replied.

"Do you know who he was called after?" he was asked.

"Of course I do," he replied, "the loveliest dog that ever

breathed. There are three here. How is John?" he asked.

John was the sitter's nephew.

He told her that her sister was there, and also a woman named Margaret Allen. He referred to some automatic writing that he gives through a friend of hers, and discussed, very naturally, matters of common interest to them.

Then he made way for Margaret Allen, a very determined personality.

Margaret Allen told this sitter all about her dogs who had died. She gave all their names.

When Red Cloud followed her, he said the dogs were still alive. The love showered upon them by human beings gave them sustenance. In the animal spheres they grew upon love.

"The love you give dogs and cats puts a soul into being," he explained. "The friendship of a dog, the love of a dumb animal can teach human beings something sometimes. Hold on!"

Then came a voice which spoke to Mary Glynne:

"Aunt Laura speaking," she said.

"I did not expect to talk to you," said Mary Glynne.

"Dennis brought me here and your dear father," was the reply.

Dennis, of course, was Dennis Neilson-Terry, the husband of Mary Glynne.

"Aunt Laura," asked Miss Glynne, "do you know what I did for you this year?"

"Yes. You put some flowers on my grave."

Miss Glynne told me afterwards this was very remarkable. When she was in South Africa with her husband, she made a special journey to Port Elizabeth to find her aunt's grave and put some flowers on it.

"I had better send Dennis in," said her Aunt Laura.

"Give Mother my love and tell her I am very much alive."

"Hullo, darling," said a male voice immediately.

Dennis Neilson-Terry had a long and intimate conversation with his wife, far too intimate to be recorded here.

He sent a message for his sister, Phyllis Neilson-Terry, and also a message for his father. Although he had spoken once before in this circle, Red Cloud explained he was still too tense.

"You see, little lady," he said to Mary Glynne, your little man was very well known. Therefore it was easy for Red Cloud to find him.

"But Red Cloud would much rather find your Aunt Laura. The medium might have known Dennis Neilson-Terry, but she could not know about your Aunt Laura."

The last communicator to speak was Sir Henry Segrave. He greeted his wife, and spoke to two sitters seated next to her.

One was his brother, whom he greeted as "Rod," his name being Rodney, and his brother's wife, whom he called by her name. He spoke to all three, sending messages to friends.

Although it was the first time that Sir Henry's brother and his wife had ever been to a voice séance, they told me it was the most amazing experience they had ever had in their lives.

Lady Segrave had often described her talks with her husband, but they did not realise how wonderful and how natural they were.

Then came Red Cloud's final peroration.

"You are losing the Old Year and the New Year is swinging in. Let the New Year be like an open book.

"Let the great love of the spirit teach you all to understand each other, knowing the first great law of tolerance one to another, learning that song of old as taught by the Nazarene, 'Blessed are ye when men shall revile ye and persecute ye.'

"Remember all those things the Nazarene taught you, and in remembering them you will understand the laws.

"Open up your hearts and respond to the music of your God. Grant unto all men peace upon earth, unto all peoples the necessaries of life, the at-oneness with your Maker.

"In so doing, let the next year respond to the voice of the spirit and so help your dark old world to light. God bless you all."

SIR WILLIAM SEFTON BRANKER COMES BACK
[13th January, 1933]

"SEFTON BRANCKER speaking. I want to speak to M—**."

It was the voice of Sir William Sefton Brancker, the former Director of Civil Aviation to the British Air Ministry, asking for Ronald M—**, an inventor, whom he said he was trying to assist.

Ten spirit voices addressed their friends and relatives in the circle with Red Cloud interposing, as usual, his comments of wisdom and helpfulness.

"Kate," said one of the first voices. "It is John Norris. Here I am. Trying to speak to you, my wife." "Yes, sweetheart," came the answer.

"I am not far away from you, dear," he told her. "Do you know who is here with me?"

"Your father, William, and Emily your mother," was the reply. "Do you know who else is here?"

"No."

"Mrs. Simmons," the spirit voice told her.

John Norris then asked to be remembered to "Mary, your sister," and "Annie," another sister.

"How is your chest?" he was asked by his wife. "It doesn't sound better."

"It is all right now," he told her. "Do you remember how

** *Names and references suppressed by the author.*

the blood choked me? Haemorrhage."

"Yes," she answered. "Are you happy now, darling?"

"How can I be happy without you? I am so glad to be able to come here."

Then very excitedly he shouted, "Can you hear my voice?" He had succeeded in reproducing his actual voice.

Red Cloud followed immediately and said, "That is the first time he has spoken in the direct voice, and, considering that he died of haemorrhage, I think he did very well."

"This is Betty speaking," volunteered another communicator. "I want my father and mother. Betty Cardew speaking. Hullo, Daddy."

Her parents were excited.

"It is so splendid to get through to you. Alan is here with me," went on the child, offering another piece of evidence.

"I have been excited all day," Betty said, "hoping I should be able to speak to you. Daddy, I love you so much, and Mummy, too," she added.

"George is here, and I have brought the boy with me. Can you hear me, dear?" she asked.

She was so anxious to know whether her voice was audible to them.

"Quite clearly," they told her.

"It is so wonderful to hear your voices," Betty said. "You have come such a long way. I am so glad you won't be disappointed."

"We would go much further," was the reply.

"I heard you playing the organ the other day," Betty told them. "It made me so happy."

Betty discussed with her mother her gift of automatic writing, and told her, "I write through your hand."

"Alan asked me to give you all his love," she said, "and so did George and Emily. Don't grieve for me.

"When you go to church, Daddy, I don't mean the Spiritualist church—you go to Bournemouth, don't you—just remember Betty is by your side when you play the organ."

"God bless you," were her parting words.

"Frederick Gorle speaking. I want Gertie," came clearly from the trumpet.

"Yes, dear. What are you going to say?" he was asked.

"Gertie dear, I am so pleased with what you did with my books," he told her, revealing his interest in his belongings. "Send some to a good library—the Morris Library."

"I will have to find out where that is," she said.

Frederick Gorle gave her some advice about relatives, and told her, "I like that statue of St. Francis of Assisi that you put on my grave. It is very beautiful."

"I thought you would like it," she answered. Then followed a long conversation, full of intimate details and advice, including messages for members of the family.

An Indian guide spoke to his medium. He gave his name and told her all about her journey from Ireland, and gave her messages to pass on to others whom she knew.

He also gave her some advice about her mediumship.

"Father," a young voice said through the trumpet.

"It is Theodore Reeves speaking."

"Yes, I hear you, Theodore," said his father.

"I am so pleased to hear you," came the answer.

"Where is Mother?"

"She wanted to be here," he was told, " but she is not well. She sends her love to you."

"Why didn't you bring Doll?" asked the spirit voice.

"She is not well."

"How is Eric?" he enquired. "This is the first time I have spoken. Uncle David is here with me, and half a dozen of your relatives are here. There are Uncle Edward, your cousin Polly, and Aunt Emily."

"Give them all my love," said Mr. Reeves. "I always remember Aunt Emily and her kindness to me as a boy."

"And Jimmy Walters is here," the spirit son went on. "Somebody else is coming to speak to you now, Dad, but please tell Eric I am helping him all I can.

"Tell Mother Uncle Tom is here. Listen, Father, this is evidence. Tell Mother that her mother Elizabeth and your mother Anne are here. Good night, Dad. There is someone else coming for you."

There were some whisperings through the trumpet, and a voice was heard to say, "Just a moment. I must get accustomed to it. This is more marvellous than I anticipated."

Then he gave his name, "The Rev. Alfred Woodnut speaking."

"My wife's uncle," volunteered Mr. Reeves.

"It is only a few months since I passed," the voice went on.

"That is quite right."

"Shall I tell you the date? The 30th August, that was when I left my body."

"Yes," said Mr. Reeves.

"It is more marvellous than I thought, my boy, to have this wonderful privilege of talking to you. You see, I was very much an orthodox clergyman."

"Have you changed a little in your views?" asked Mr. Reeves.

"Yes, yes; one must. I never expected this. It is a revelation, a revelation. What a pity I was not more understanding of the great truth of immortality."

"You understood quite a lot."

"Yes," said the spirit clergyman, "but I was bound by the Thirty-nine Articles. I thank God that I am allowed to speak, to add my little confirmation of the truth."

"Herbert Watson," announced the next spirit voice.

The friend to whom he was speaking wanted to make sure, and she began to ask him a series of questions.

"Can you remember the name of the book you gave me?" was one of them.

The voice laughed. "I believe she is going to cross-question me," he said.

He steadily went on with his messages, giving names of friends, but still the cross-examination persisted.

"All right," said Herbert Watson. "I will start on you."

"Who are you?" he asked. "How do I know you are who you say you are? Who gave you the right to come here? Why did you drag me up from the dead? Now do you recognise me?"

The sitters roared with laughter.

The next voice to speak was that of Dennis Neilson-Terry, the actor, who has already spoken on previous occasions, both to his wife, Mary Glynne, who was present this evening, and his sister, Phyllis Neilson-Terry.

He had a long conversation with Mary Glynne, in the course of which he told her, "I have brought some flowers for you."

This was a remarkable piece of evidence, although it sounded a common-place statement.

At a sitting with a medium, held on the previous

Wednesday, where she spoke to her husband, Mary Glynne had asked him to tell her what he would say at the next voice sitting.

"I will come through and say, 'I have brought you some flowers,'" he said.

He had kept his word, and furnished his wife with another link in the proof of his survival.

Then Sir William Sefton Brancker spoke.

Ronald M—**, who had met him on earth, easily recognised his voice, as did another sitter.

He explained to Mr. M—** that he was interested in his patent which concerned aviation, but although there were still one or two points which he had not achieved, they would soon be accomplished.

"On no account must you give in," he told him. "You are experimenting with things that are going to be helpful to the world, and also to flying."

"Yes," said the inventor, "I will do my best to have more patience. I wish you were here, though. We shall never be able to replace you."

"Oh, no," came the reply, "there are plenty of good men."

Sir Henry Segrave spoke for some minutes to his wife.

Then came Doctor "B. G.," one of the frequent communicators, who spoke to his friend, Mrs. Alice Liddell.

"B. G." assists Red Cloud in his healing work and sent a long message to his band of healers.

When he had finished, Red Cloud told us the circle must be brought to an end.

** *Names and references suppressed by the author.*

SIR THOMAS LIPTON SPEAKS, SÉANCE REPLY TO A PRAYER
[10th February, 1933]

"I AM Bessy Manning, and I want you to send a message to my mother."

This request was made to me by a spirit voice at this séance.

Bessy Manning came half-way through the sitting.

Red Cloud, addressing me, said, "This child has approached me to get contact with her mother. She will give her own evidence."

Then we heard a voice saying, "I will, all right, I will. . ."

"Come along," I said, encouraging the voice to speak. "You are going to give me a message. Come and talk to us."

"I will, if I am allowed to talk," came the voice. "A kind man brought me here."

Then she gave us her name, Bessy Manning, with the message to be sent to her mother.

"I suppose I must tell you where she lives," she said. "Listen, I will try." Slowly and distinctly came the address— I4 Canterbury Street, Blackburn.

"My name is Bessy Manning," she repeated. "I died with tuberculosis last Easter. I have brought my brother, who was killed by a motor. Mother has prayed because she reads your paper** and has asked that some day, the great guide Red

** *This was a reference to the Psychic News, Spiritualist newspaper, that the author edits, where references to Red Cloud had been made.*

Cloud would bring me here and her to me."

"I will send a message to your mother tomorrow," I told Bessy.

"Tell Mother," she said, "I still have my two long plaits. I am twenty-two, and I have got blue eyes.

Tell her I do want her to come here. Could you bring her?"

Then she added very wistfully, "She is not rich, she is poor."

"We will see if we can bring her," chimed in Hannen Swaffer.

"She is so unhappy," went on Bessy. "She says she lost both of us. You will help her, won't you?

"God will bless you if you help her. Thank you, thank you, thank you."

She was followed by Red Cloud, who said, "Even as you do it unto one of these . . ."

"Red Cloud," I said, "there must be thousands who pray like her mother."

"I have only one instrument," said Red Cloud, with a note of sadness in his voice.

It made me realise what could be achieved if there were a hundred voice mediums like Estelle Roberts.

"Will you invite her mother?" Swaffer asked.

"Will I?" answered Red Cloud. "Would you?"

You will see from the next chapter what happened when Mrs. Manning attended the voice sitting.

The first voice to speak was that of a child, who gave its name as Timmie.

Red Cloud always lets the children come first, following the teaching of the Great Teacher who said, "A little child shall lead them."

Timmie's parents were delighted to hear his voice.

"It is lovely to hear you, darling," the mother said. "Are you looking after Christopher?"

"Yes," she was told. "His eyes are splendid now. Don't get downhearted, dear. Charlie is here with me, and Gladys is here too. . . This is the first time I have been."

"It is lovely to hear your voice," Timmie was told.

"You did not think Timmie would come, did you?" was heard in reply.

Then he sent messages to some of his relatives, whose names he gave.

Timmie was followed by a spirit who gave his name as Mowbray Balme.

He spoke to somebody in the circle, whom he called Gerald, whom he wanted to convey a message of "All my love to Eileen, my wife. Thirty-eight years ago she lived with Sara Stupington. I have met Arthur Stupington over here."

Then turning to another sitter, whom he called Evie, he said, "Your father Fred Horsford is here. I am so glad to come through, I hope my pronunciation is clear. Gerald, your brother Charlie is here. This is not an easy task, and very trying for me. It is the first time."

He gave many other messages of too personal a nature to be mentioned here.

"Hold on!" came Red Cloud's voice. "There is another stranger here." He was immediately followed by a voice which said, "I want Ruth Hicks. I am Phyllis Mayby."

"I remember you," said the sitter, "and I am so glad you have come."

"I have not been here before," said Phyllis Mayby.

"My throat is quite better now. I only wish I could make my dear ones understand."

"I wish we could," said the sitter. "Can you not help Mother?"

"She does not listen," the spirit voice replied sadly. . . "Tell her to come here and talk to me. Your dear dad brought me here. He brought me because I was downhearted."

"Can we do anything more than we have been doing?" the sitter enquired.

"Only make Mother understand," was the reply.

"I would be so happy if you could. Tell her my throat is better."

The next voice asked for "Emma, Emma."

A woman seated next to me replied, "I am here. Who is that speaking?"

"I am Philip Cunliffe Owen, your father," was the reply.

After the sitting I had a long chat with the sitter who was addressed, Mrs. Emma Cunliffe Owen, the woman who raised the Sportsmen's Battalion in the war. She told me she instantly recognised her father's voice.

"Pater dear," she said, "I am glad you have come."

"Do you know who is with me?" he asked. "Let me tell you, darling. Don't give your evidence away. Edward, your husband, in other words, your first cousin. Now dear, listen."

"Yes," said the sitter.

"There are also here, grandfather Charles, Agnes, and Jenny. I want to help you. . . I have brought Dorothy with me. She will speak to you when I have finished. Also there is Alexandra, Henry, Frank, and little Clare. You remember Clare, don't you?

"I have brought them all along," he went on.

"Dorothy particularly wants to speak to you. I have been to see Hugo, my son. . . I want to send Dorothy to you. Poor

Dorothy, her end was very distressing. Do you remember the mortuary? It was a terrible shock, and you were very brave."

"Yes," said Mrs. Cunliffe Owen. "It was a terrible shock."

"Why on earth did you go and make that terrible mistake?" the spirit voice asked. "You know what I mean."

"I ought not to have done it," was the answer. "I was old enough to know better."

"You certainly were, my child," her father agreed.

There were lots of intimate details like these, a natural conversation between the living and the dead.

Then there came a voice which said to the same sitter, "Well, well, well! You, of all people, to find here! Do you know who is talking to you? Tommy Lipton!"

Mrs. Cunliffe Owen was taken by surprise.

"Fancy you being here," she said.

"Why not?" was the reply of the spirit voice.

"But you did not believe in this?"

"Never mind," said the voice. "I will prove to you who I am. Thank you for what you did."

Turning to the rest of the circle, he said, "She decorated the carriage in which my body was brought home."

"You did so much for other people," said Mrs. Owen, "I thought I would like to do something for you."

"It was very kind of you," the Lipton voice insisted. If I had known a little more, I would have left things very differently. But I was told a different story."

"I am glad you left Ossidge as a home of rest for the nurses," said the sitter.

"I am delighted to speak," Lipton said. "I want you to know I appreciate what you did. . . What was the colour? Purple cloth and laurels. And you put the yellow chrysanthemums on yourself. It was jolly nice of you."

"How are you, Sir Thomas?" asked Hannen Swaffer. "They called me out of bed to write your obituary notice."

"Did they?" was the reply. "Well, tell them I am not dead, Swaffer."

"I am sorry they would not allow me to see you when you were ill," Mrs. Cunliffe Owen told him.

"Never mind, never mind," was the reply.

Here Mrs. Treloar asked the sitter if what Sir Thomas said was evidential.

"Every word," was her reply.

She was yet to have some more evidence.

The next voice addressed her, saying, "Mother, I am Dorothy. What a terrible death!"

"I know it was, darling, and I could do nothing." "I was just struck down," said the spirit voice. "Are you happier now, darling? her mother asked. "Yes, now I am," Dorothy replied. "But it was all so terrible."

"Still, it was a long time ago. Try and forget."

"Don't grieve for me, Mother darling," the spirit voice told her. "You have these gifts (the reference was to her mother's psychic gifts). Why don't you use them?"

"I am not sufficiently developed," her mother replied. "I am still looking for those things."

"You mean the papers, don't you? I will help you."

Dorothy gave her the name of a solicitor who she said had the papers in his possession. She also gave her mother certain advice on how to proceed in connection with this affair.

It was a long conversation, which, like many others in the séance-room, contained details of too intimate a nature to be recorded in a book.

Red Cloud, who followed, said, "You people sometimes ask for evidence. I tell you something that only the mother knows. That little baby Clare of yours was only three days old when she passed. I tell you something about her. Did you know . .?" and he added a most intimate reference to the child's internal organs, one that caused her passing.

"Yes, I did," said the mother.

"All right," replied Red Cloud. "As long as you knew. Now then what do you think of that?"

Then there was an amusing incident.

"Is there a gentleman over by the door?" asked Red Cloud.

"Do you mean me?" asked one of the sitters.

"Yes. Will you ask your little lady friend to keep quiet?"

"What is her name?" enquired the sitter.

"I don't know her name," said Red Cloud, "but she is spoiling all the vibrations. Ask her to keep quiet."

"What shall I do? " asked the sitter. "Shall I threaten her or cajole her?"

Then he addressed the invisible disturber. "Keep quiet," he said. "Don't get excited."

"You could not get her to do it on earth," Red Cloud told him.

"Impossible," answered the sitter. "I know you have a bit of a job."

"I asked her to keep quiet," Red Cloud told him. "She is a very nice, sweet lady, but what a temper!" "I think I recognise her."

"She says, ' I don't want a damn Indian to tell me what to do.' She is natural, and I would rather have her natural, because she has a fine soul. You sit there and send out thoughts to her to keep her quiet."

The sitter said the "Indian" phrase exactly summed her up.

Many other voices spoke to us that night. There was one who said, "I want to get through to my sister if I can. Her name is Pearce. I am her brother, George Pearce."

A few minutes' conversation bridged the gulf of death, as brother and sister spoke to each other again. He encouraged her to send messages to his mother. A spirit, who had only passed on a few weeks before, returned to speak to his wife, giving her advice about her three children.

And so the living voices of the dead spoke to us. The last to speak was, as usual, Sir Henry Segrave, who spoke to his wife.

On the following day, without the slightest doubt in my mind that Bessy Manning's message might be incorrect, I sent a telegram to her mother at the address given. I said, "Your daughter Bessy spoke to us at Red Cloud's circle last night."

As I did not receive a reply to my telegram, I wired her again.

I received two letters from Mrs. Manning, which read:

"I don't know whom I have to thank for the great joy you have given me. I thank you with all my heart and soul for the telegram I received last Saturday.

"I wanted to shout it from, the house-tops. I laughed and cried all at once. . . "What a wonderful spirit Red Cloud is, and how good and kind you all are. I feel sure you will carry your kindness further and let me know what my Bessy said.

"Oh, the glorious happiness to me and mine. . . How can I ever thank you enough? That bit of paper is more to me than untold gold.

"I will pray with all my heart for all of you. . .

"You will tell me, won't you, if she sent me a little message.

It is a wonderful, glorious truth, and again I thank you so much. Also my husband and my other two daughters thank you."

In her second letter she said:

"I have received your second telegram. I am sorry to have caused you to have to send a second one, and I am so thankful for your wonderful kindness. You could not have received my letter which I posted on Sunday.

"I was very upset not being able to send you a return telegram, as things are not very bright at present. I want you to understand how grateful we all are. We would do anything possible to repay your great goodness. You don't know what it means to us.

"My daughter passed on last Easter Monday, and my son was killed nearly nine years ago. Had it not been for getting in touch with a Spiritualist family, I would have been raving mad.

"I am longing to know what Bessy said, and if it is your wish to print it, you may do so. I want to comfort others as I have been. . .

"It must be great to hear Mrs. Estelle Roberts and the other great ones. I wish I had the glorious gift. Again, I thank you so very much."

No theories of telepathy or "sub-conscious mind" can apply to this evidence. No suggestion of fraud or collusion can be entertained.

Mrs. Manning had never seen Estelle Roberts in her life, neither had she ever had any correspondence with her.

Yet a full name and address were transmitted, and a complete message given, every detail of which was accurate.

MRS. MANNING TALKS TO HER DEAD DAUGHTER
[24th February, 1933]

I HAD arranged to meet Mrs. Manning at St. Pancras station, where her train was due to arrive at 6.10 that evening. I took her down to Teddington, where the circle meets, and there for the first time she met Mrs. Estelle Roberts.

Mrs. Manning told me she had never been in London in her life.

The séance that night began with the voice of Jackie, which was immediately recognised by the regular sitters.

Then there came a spirit voice which said very clearly, "I want to send a message, if I can. I want to talk to a lady here."

"Which lady do you want? "asked Mrs. Treloar.

"Mrs. Olsen," replied the voice. "This is Crosby speaking. I want you to give a message to Win Fisher for me. Tell her I was dazed by my passing, but I am managing very successfully to manipulate my new body."

"I will tell her," said Mrs. Olsen.

"Did you know the spirit voice?" she was asked.

"No," the sitter replied, "but I know Win Fisher, who is a great friend of mine."

"Hold on!" came the voice of Red Cloud. "There is a stranger here."

A few seconds later, there came through the trumpet a voice which said, "I am going to try. I am trying to talk. I am Cynthia Cawthorpe."

"Yes, I know you," said one of the sitters.

"That is why I came," the spirit voice replied. "Thank you so much for your kind thoughts. Your guide brought me here to talk to you, but I find it very difficult. . .

"Give my love to my mother," she added. "Tell her not to grieve for me. I am much happier now that the pain has gone. God bless you, dear. Pray for me, won't you?"

The sitter was amazed at this communication. "She was a sweet girl of nineteen," she volunteered. "She only passed over about three weeks ago, in terrible pain."

Then Red Cloud spoke again, and told us to help the next spirit, a little child.

"Be patient with her," he said, "and leave her to give her own evidence."

"Mother, Mother!" we heard a child's voice calling through the trumpet.

"Is your mother here?" asked Mrs. Treloar.

"Yes," the voice replied. I want my mother. Her name is Lack. My daddy brought me here. Mother darling!" she called.

Her mother answered. Then the child gave her evidence.

"Do you remember how they took me to the window to revive me," she said, "and I got pneumonia?"

She also gave many intimate details of her death, satisfying from the point of view of evidence to her mother, but they cannot be recorded here.

"I am happy now I have told you," the child said. "I wanted you to know I was happy. Daddy is here with me—Daddy Ben. Do you know who helped me to come tonight?" she asked. Then she gave the name, Dr. Franz Hoffman. "You know him, don't you, Mummy?" she added.

Still more evidence was to follow.

"Why did you come here as Miss Lack," she asked, "when you are Mrs. Aladar?"

"This is the most wonderful piece of evidence," the mother exclaimed. "Darling, you know why."

"Yes, I know," her daughter answered. "You wanted to know if I knew."

"It is very difficult to talk," we heard coming through the trumpet. "I want to talk, but I am afraid I shall not be able to do so."

"You are talking now," I told this spirit voice. "We can hear you quite distinctly."

"I want to talk to a young friend here," the voice continued, "who has been very kindly helping my wife. His name is D'Albert."

"Yes," said Edward D'Albert, who was present in the séance-room. "Who are you?"

"You require my name," was the reply. "Well, here goes— Charles Augustus Edmund Trevor Batty."

"Yes," said Mr. D'Albert, "quite right."

"How is Spot?" the voice asked. (Spot was the name of his dog.)

The spirit voice also enquired after somebody named Hugo.

"Do you know what happened to him?" asked the sitter.

"Yes, I do," was the reply. "He got married."

"Can you give a message for Mrs. Trevor Batty?" he was asked.

"Give her all my love, my boy. I am so grateful to you for the help you have given her. . . You have tried to give her a little light in her hour of sorrow. Tell my dear wife," he added, "that Spot sees me."

There was a long conversation between them, other messages being sent to the "Hugo" mentioned and to the wife.

Mr. D'Albert tried to thank Red Cloud for the evidence that had been brought to him, but Red Cloud, as usual, would accept no thanks. He made his inevitable reply. "Don't thank me, thank God."

The difficulties in describing the happenings of the night are accentuated by the fact that I have to censor so much that is said by the spirit voices which would hurt the feelings of other people who are involved.

There was one communicator, who gave her name and referred to a relative still living to whom she had left her money. She told the sitter that this man had spent it all in drink.

"He drank and drank," she said, "until it was all gone."

Then there spoke to us one of the regular communicators, a spirit son who always speaks to his mother when she is present.

He told her how he had the greatest laugh of his life when he saw the two dogs chewing up his sister's false teeth.

He was followed by a spirit voice announcing itself as "Eugene Ouida."

"Listen," said the voice, "I saw you lunching with Mother and Louise."

"Yes, that is quite true," said a Mrs. Hulme, who was being addressed.

"I was attached to the Cornwall Light Infantry," the spirit voice went on. "Tell Mother I have returned. I should just love to speak to her. Tell her," he added, "it was impossible for anyone here to have known about me."

"This is wonderful," Mrs. Hulme told Red Cloud.

"It is not wonderful," was the reply. "Only the truth—the truth that shall set you free."

The next voice insisted, "I am going to talk, if I can. I want to talk to my son, Alfred Jenkinson."

"I am here," was the reply.

"I have a great difficulty in explaining myself, because there are two Alfreds and two Marys."

"That is quite right, Father," his son told him.

"I and my wife were Alfred and Mary," the spirit voice explained, "and my boy's wife's father and mother were Alfred and Mary, too; and so we have a difficulty, when we speak, to try and make them understand who we are... This is the biggest truth of all, that God ever gave to humanity."

Then he added one more piece of evidence. "You have got my scissors in your pocket," he told his son.

The spirit father gave him some advice about an old business, which he wanted him to begin all over again. It was advice totally unexpected by the sitter.

"Remember, when you go back to the Bay," he said, "I shall go back with you." (His son told me that he lived at Colwyn Bay.) "My boy," he added, "I should love you to see the gardens over here. You know how I love gardening. It was my lifetime's work."

"Hullo, hullo, hullo," came a spirit voice loudly through the trumpet.

"Hullo," answered Mrs. Treloar. "Will you tell us who you are? "

"I would like to know your name first," the spirit voice replied.

"My name is Treloar," she told the voice. "Will you give

me your name? "

"Yes," was the answer. "I am Captain Bert Allen. Now we know each other."

"Good evening, Captain," said one of the sitters, addressing him. "I thought, somehow, you would come tonight."

Captain Allen told his friend about a message he had given to be passed on to one of his relatives.

"I know," he said, "that you were laughed at for your pains. I want to thank you for the work you have been doing in helping others at Bristol.

"I have got your father James here," he said. "There is also a lady named Elizabeth. Harry is here with Liz—that is, your sister and brother-in-law.

"Do you know what your father said to me?" he asked. "Just give my daughter Emily all my love. This is a wonderful circle."

Then, addressing us all, the spirit voice said, "You see, I understood a little of this."

I was told afterwards that Captain Bert Allen was one of the founders of a Spiritualist church at Bristol.

Bessy Manning then spoke to her mother. "Ma," she said, "it is Bessy speaking."

"Yes, Bessy," replied her mother.

The spirit daughter was full of excitement. So much so, that half-way through her conversation the trumpet dropped, an indication that she could not hold the "power."

"Bessy," her mother said, "this is wonderful. You know how your mother loves you, don't you?"

"It is wonderful," Bessy replied. "God bless you, Ma. Tell Father not to worry. Tommy is here, too," she went on. "We are here together. Tommy is also anxious to speak to you, Ma.

It is so wonderful, I don't know how to talk. I am so excited."

"Don't get excited, love," her mother answered. "Talk to Mother. Do you come into the home, Bessy? "

"You know I do," was the reply. "I try to talk to you there. Day after day, you talk to my picture. You stand in front of it, you pick it up and kiss it, and I watch you all the time.

"You were telling Father about his boots this morning, weren't you, Ma?" she said.

"That is quite right, Bessy," her mother told her.

"You said they wanted mending, didn't you, Ma?" the spirit voice continued.

"I understand what you mean, Bessy," she was told.

"My ma. I called her Ma," said Bessy.

In repeating the words of Bessy, so as to enable the stenographer to get it down correctly, I thought, once, she said "Mother." I was instantly reproved by the spirit voice, who corrected me, saying, "Ma."

Bessy Manning told her mother that she (the mother) was wearing her beads on her neck. "It was a big shock for you when Tommy was killed," she said.

"She brought the boy Tommy with her," Red Cloud added, when Bessy had left. "He is named after his father."

Right at the end, the spirit voice of Sir Henry Segrave spoke to his wife in his usual inimitable fashion.

Then Red Cloud announced he would have to bring the séance to a close. Even then, he made way for a few minutes to allow a spirit communicator to give a promised message to one of the sitters.

When he returned, Red Cloud also gave Shaw Desmond, one of the sitters that night, a message from one of his relatives on the Other Side.

"So we pass a fleeting hour," Red Cloud said. "And now I go. All of you that seek shall find, if you but realise behind the darkness is the light of understanding. Good night, everybody."

The trumpet dropped. The séance was over.

"I am the happiest woman in the world," Mrs. Manning told me afterwards.

Yes, it had all been worth while, if only one person had had proved to her beyond doubt that her daughter was not dead, but still living.

A few days later, Mrs. Manning wrote me the following letter:

MRS MANNING'S LETTER

"I am writing this for the comfort of others, knowing I shall be ridiculed by some, laughed at by a few, but blessed by many.

"My only son, whom I adored, was killed by a motor. He was a dear little chap, who loved me very dearly. I was frantic—utterly crushed.

"I lost all hope. All my ambitions lay buried in his grave. When life was darkest, I became acquainted with a Spiritualist family who saved my reason. These people told me things that set me thinking. Under their instructions, I got messages from him.

"Eight years later, my daughter Bessy passed on, one of the most lovable and sweetest girls who ever lived.

"Just before the end, she said, 'Mother, if it is possible at all, I will come back.'

"I knew she would keep that promise. She has come in the most unexpected manner. I had often heard of the Red Cloud circle.

"It came as a big surprise to me to receive a telegram from Mr. Barbanell telling me my daughter had come through, asking for her mother and telling them where she lived.

"I was astonished and overjoyed at the news. Through the kindness of Mr. Barbanell, Mr. Hannen Swaffer and Mrs. Estelle Roberts, it was made possible for me to go to London and attend the circle.

"It was a great experience. Everywhere I was met with kindness. I heard many spirit voices, and all were recognised. It was most amazing.

"I heard my own daughter speaking to me, in the same old loving way, and the selfsame peculiarities of speech. She spoke of incidents that I know for a positive fact no other person could know. I, her mother, am the best judge, and I swear before Almighty God it was Bessy.

"She told me she had brought her brother with her, told of him being killed and gave his name. She spoke of many things that have passed in our home, things that were far from my mind at the time.

"I thank God, with all my heart and soul. He answered my prayers, and I have prayed, long and often.

"I have no fear of so-called death. I am looking forward to the glorious meeting with all my loved ones."

FIFTEEN spirit voices spoke to us at the voice circle.

The first one to address us was Jackie.

"You are the door-opener, aren't you, Jackie?" his foster-mother said to him.

"Yes," he replied. "What would Red Cloud do without me?"

Then there came through the trumpet, "Wallie. It is Willie speaking. Do you know whom I have brought here tonight? Joyce. She is going to speak to you. . . Listen, Wallie. I knew it was your wish to see me before I passed out."

"Yes, it was," he was told.

"You tried to get leave," the spirit voice said, "but you had to go up the line. You know, it was a bad one I got in the leg."

"I did not know," his friend replied, "but I have heard it since."

"It is fine to see you, Wallie," the voice said. "Can you hear me?"

Wallie also sent several messages to his friends whom he named and gave a warning that one of his relatives would soon pass over.

"Cheer up," were his last words. "It is nice to talk to you again. I am going to send Joyce to you now. Listen and talk to her. I am going to push her in. All the best. . ."

"Hold on!" came the voice of Red Cloud. "A little child

shall lead them. . ."

Then there came a child's voice, distinctly calling, "Daddy. Joycie speaking. Can you hear me, Daddy?"

"Yes, Joycie, quite well," said her father.

"Will you kiss my Donnie for me?" Joycie asked.

I repeated this message, so that the stenographer could understand. I thought that Joyce said "Dolly." She immediately corrected me.

"No. No. I did not say that. I said, 'My Donnie, my brother.'"

"Yes. I know, Joyce," said her father.

"Millicent, my sister, is here," she continued. "I am so happy. I have brought Uncle Willie with me. Tell Mummy I came here. I am ten years old. . . Millicent did not have diphtheria like me."

"No. I know, Joyce," her father confirmed.

The sound of kisses was heard coming through the trumpet.

Then Joyce's voice was heard again.

"Don't cry, Daddy," she said. "I am so happy. Be happy, Daddy."

"I will, darling," her father answered.

"Come and talk to Joycie again," the spirit voice said. "Don't cry, Daddy," she repeated. "All the people here love you and you love Joycie too. I will come back again someday."

"I am sure you will, my sweetheart," said her father.

"Good night, my daddy darling," were her last words. "Kiss Donnie and Mummy, and give my love to Granny."

The trumpet moved towards my friend Mrs. Fulcher, who was seated on my right. "Kit," said the voice. It was her husband, calling her by her nickname, who had spoken to her once before in this séance-room.

There was a long conversation between husband and wife, in which I joined. I can testify that it was his voice which spoke.

When I asked him whom his grandson was named after, he replied laughingly, "Yes - me. Are you trying to pull my leg?"

There followed a pathetic scene.

"Mother," said a voice sadly. "I want my mother."

"Can you find your mother?" asked Mrs. Treloar.

"Yes," was the reply, as she touched her mother with the trumpet. "Mother darling. Try to listen to me."

"I will try," her mother answered, her voice choked with sobs.

"Don't be unhappy about me," the spirit daughter said. "I love you just the same. I was so glad you went to Ingerborg."

"Oh, my darling!" exclaimed her mother. "What a piece of evidence. What conditions did you find yourself in when you died?"

"It was all so strange and quick," the spirit voice replied. "You know, twenty-four hours."

"Yes," her mother said sadly, "it was only one hour before you died that I knew you were ill."

"I did not know I had a duodenal ulcer," the spirit voice told her, "and peritonitis set in."

"No one knew you had anything the matter with you," her mother said. "Did anybody meet you?" "Yes," was the reply, "your mother."

The spirit daughter said that she used her foreign languages on the Other Side, and that she worked for the League of Nations when on earth.

Her mother was distressed during the whole of the

conversation, and the voice asked us to try to comfort her.

"Do not cry for me, Mummy," she said, as she implored us all to help.

"You people help her," she said. "She is so lonely. Tell my mother I am quite happy."

When she left, Red Cloud said, "She was thirty-six years old."

"Yes, that is true," the sitter said. "She was thirty-six just a few days before she died."

"She did not die," came Red Cloud's quick response.

Here Shaw Desmond suggested, "I think everything they did here they do there, Red Cloud."

"Yes, even live," was Red Cloud's answer.

The next spirit voice called for "Lulu," addressing Louise Owen.

"Kitty speaking," she said. "Darling, I am so happy."

"I looked at your picture before I came away," said Louise Owen, "hoping you would come and talk to me."

"My dear, of course I would," the spirit voice replied. "You knew I would try. I am quite close to you. How are they all at home?"

Louise Owen was very excited. Kitty was her sister.

"I think I am the luckiest woman alive," she volunteered.

"I think I am the luckiest woman to be allowed to speak," her spirit sister instantly replied.

"Say good evening to Mr. Swaffer. . . Do you know Lottie (Swaffer's spirit sister-in-law) is helping me."

"You know," said Swaffer, "it was Louise who brought me into this."

"Yes," said the voice of Kitty, "and you are bringing Lulu into it tonight, aren't you?"

Kitty was followed by a voice very excitedly giving the name of Bernard and asking for a Mr. Shelley. He was so excited that he could hardly speak. After a minute or two, he dropped the trumpet. The next communication was very impressive.

"Mother," we heard a despairing voice call through the trumpet.

"Can you see your mother?" asked Mrs. Treloar.

"Mother," the voice went on, "it is Joe P—** speaking. Can you hear me, Mother? Listen, dear, I did not want to leave you. It was dreadful for me to do it, but I did not understand. Mother, she broke my heart."

"I know, darling," his mother said. The spirit voice then described how he committed suicide.

Although he gave his name I have, for obvious reasons, deleted it from this record.

"I will always love you, Mother," the spirit voice said, comforting and reassuring his distressed parent. "I am going to France with you. I am going to stay with you. Never again will anyone break my heart. . .

"I have forgiven her. Mother dear, the doctors told me over here that my suicide was caused through my head. It was injured in birth. Mother dear, be happy. I love you. I love you. I love you."

"Yes, dear," she told him. "I know, and I love you."

"Don't let the world think wrongly of me," the voice told her.

"No, dear," came the reply. "What the world thinks does not matter."

"I want you not to grieve for me," the spirit son said. "I am always with you, all the time. Don't cry. . . God is good. He

** *Names and references suppressed by the author.*

has allowed me to speak to you to tell you I did not understand. God bless you, darling Mother. God bless you."

Red Cloud, who followed, comforted the sitter with words of gentle wisdom.

"Your world called it temporary insanity," he said, "and yet it was nothing of the sort. The boy's skull was injured in birth. There was pressure on the grey matter, caused by haemorrhage, and then something snapped and you blame him. Keep your courage, Mother, and smile. He is not dead."

Red Cloud asked me to give some messages to some friends of mine, a Mr. and Mrs. Tinling, who were present.

He explained that the spirit who wished to speak was very shy. A message was given in symbolic form, which was quickly appreciated by Mr. Tinling. Some nicknames were also mentioned.

Then there came a spirit voice which said firmly and distinctly, "You do not recognise me, I presume?"

"Who is it?" we asked.

Louise Owen, however, had quickly detected the personality of her Chief, Lord Northcliffe.

The spirit voice, however, refused to be greeted as Lord Northcliffe, but insisted on being called Alfred Harmsworth. "Titles mean nothing over here," he said.

"I thought it was you," said Shaw Desmond.

"Yes," replied the Northcliffe voice, "being fey, you would."

"The futility of it all," the Northcliffe voice continued. "War and starvation. Are you binding yourselves together in unity and strength? Or are you all standing in groups? It is so futile, if you don't all get together and accomplish something."

"You can go on talking," said Hannen Swaffer. "I have had to listen to a good many lectures by you."

"If you were all banded together," the Northcliffe voice went on, "instead of a gathering here and a gathering there— it is a waste of time. What you want to do is to get together and do something for the world to avert war."

"But what shall we do, Chief?" asked Swaffer.

"Can you not get together?" came the reply.

"What would we do if we got together?" Swaffer asked.

"Talk," was the brief reply.

Swaffer persisted: "And then what?"

"Act," the spirit said.

Here Shaw Desmond intervened. "Suppose we called a meeting at the Albert Hall for peace," he said. "Would that help?"

"The trouble is," repeated Northcliffe, "you are not sufficiently united."

"You do not understand," Swaffer insisted. "The Spiritualist movement is not a Pacifist movement. They won't listen."

"Then you are all a lot of fools," was Northcliffe's comment.

"War is caused by economic facts," Swaffer said. "We have to alter the circumstances."

"If we tell the world, will they listen to us?" asked Shaw Desmond.

"Struggle until they do," Northcliffe answered.

Swaffer was still not satisfied. "Society is mixed up in armaments today," he pointed out. "Are you going to abolish Aldershot and Portsmouth?"

"Get at the roots," was Northcliffe's reply.

"They won't listen," said Swaffer.

"Then they are all a damn lot of fools," the spirit remarked.

The Northcliffe voice was followed by a spirit who, when asked by her friend what she was doing in the spirit world, replied very amusingly, "Playing golf. Who have you got with you?" the voice asked.

"Hazel," was the reply.

"Why do you call her Hazel," the spirit asked, "when her name is Henderson?"

She was followed by a voice giving the name of Mary Philpot. She asked to speak to her stepson.

Then there came the most amusing communicator of the evening. His replies made us roar with laughter.

It was the voice of a Cockney soldier and his humour was of the Cockney variety. His whole conversation, though, was full of evidence.

"Alf!" the voice shouted. "Do you remember me? George Ellis. Royal Warwickshire Regiment."

"Yes, that is right," said the sitter addressed. "I was out there the same time as you."

"Well you were not a bad old buddy. Ted Cole is here," the voice told him. "So is Bill Walker and old Georgie Clark. I say, your father is here—in his waistcoat with all the buttons off and his yellow canary front."

"What are you all doing over there now?" the sitter asked.

The answer convulsed us with laughter.

"Pulling your leg," was the reply.

The spirit voice told him about another friend he had brought, Dickie Brown, "the one who fell into the water trough."

"Do you remember old Archibald?" he went on. "You know, Smithy. I have got him over here. He had his arm blown off."

Then he told him about another spirit, an old soldier friend who he said still had "as long a neck as ever."

"Yes," said his friend, "that is quite right. He had a terribly long neck."

"Like a chicken," commented the spirit voice. "I say, who do you think I have seen? The old chap. Wait a minute—old General Blake. . . Do you remember we greased the soles of his boots? Cheerio. . . Old Crackers asked me to say 'Good night' for him."

"That is marvellous," the sitter told me. "The man who had a long neck had to have a special collar for his tunic."

When the Cockney soldier had gone, Red Cloud gave one more scrap of evidence to the sitter.

"Your little baby is here," he said. "Your little son who passed on. He has grown up into a man now."

For a few moments, the spirit voice of Sir Henry Segrave addressed his wife, and after a brief conversation Red Cloud announced the circle would have to come to an end.

CONCLUSION

AND now the curtain must be rung down. To those of you who have had no psychic experiences, the contents of this book may seem very strange.

I ask you to try and put on one side all old-fashioned prejudices and consider the evidence which I have presented.

Spiritualism is either a great truth or else it is a monstrous fraud.

Either the statements recorded in this book are untrue, and scores of people are engaged in a conspiracy of collusion and cheating to deceive you, or else there are described here conversations between the living and the "dead."

One figure will, I know, puzzle you throughout this book. That is Red Cloud.

I have tried hard to describe the personality of Red Cloud, but he must be heard to be fully appreciated.

At one sitting there was a man present who was not addressed by any of the voices, which is a very rare happening.

It was a foggy night, and the conditions from the séance point of view were not good. The sitting had only lasted a short time when Red Cloud said the sitting would be closed.

The goodbyes were uttered when we heard Red Cloud's voice again. He was "controlling" the medium this time, but the voice was exactly the same one that had just spoken through the trumpet.

He said he had omitted to give some instructions to one of his healers present. He gave these and asked whether there were any questions.

"Red Cloud," said one of the women present, "is there not any message for this gentleman?" referring to the man who had not been addressed by any of the voices.

"Yes," said Red Cloud immediately, "tell him both his wives are here. The second one wants him to sell the new house. It is too full of sad memories."

This rather surprised the man, but he added, "Yes, that is true. But it is difficult to sell houses. What shall I do?"

Red Cloud's reply was very characteristic. "We don't sell houses," he said. He called me by name and said, "Talk to him about treasures in Heaven."

This reminds me that the voices often betray evidence of great humanness.

At another sitting, there was present a man and his wife. The voice had spoken in a marked Cockney accent, and said he was the husband's brother.

The spirit voice was surprised that his brother lacked money. He told him it was his own fault for lending money to relatives who never repaid, even when they could afford it.

"What shall I do?" asked his brother.

"Force yer 'and, I tell yer," he answered. "Force yer 'and!"

A spirit nephew, calling himself Jock, on another occasion was talking to his uncle who was rather deaf. Every time the spirit began to speak the deaf uncle butted in. At last Jock replied, "Och! Shut up. You have come to hear me!"

I was once discussing with Red Cloud the curious attitude of the many clergymen who denied the truth of Spiritualism.

I was pointing out to him how history shows that Truth was always opposed by the very people who should have supported it.

"Yes," he said, "pity them, pity them. They have to undo all the results of the errors of their teaching. You know they have to come to us eventually."

Periodically, Red Cloud leaves his medium for a week or two to go back, as he says, into the spheres to gain additional strength. Before these departures, he generally bids farewell to his circle of earthly friends.

On the last occasion, he delivered a farewell address. Then he asked each one present to come forward.

One by one they did so. He addressed them individually by the name that he bestowed on them. To each one he gave a message in perfect poetry. The language was beautiful. It transcended the medium's mental capacity.

Again and again, I am asked about the prevalence of Red Indian guides. Why all these Indians?

I can only say that at séances all over the world you find Red Indian guides. It may be that they lived so close to Nature that their psychic faculties became highly developed, which makes them masters of psychic laws when they pass on. After all, civilisation, although it has brought us many advantages, has usually taken us further away from Nature.

You may scoff at constant references to Red Cloud, squaws, papooses and chiefs. I cannot help it. I can only record what happens. In an enquiry into such a vast subject as Spiritualism you must face all the facts.

As an example of Red Cloud's inspiring teaching, he closed a voice séance one night with:

The glory of life is to love,
Not to be loved;
To give, not to get
To serve, not to be served;
To be a strong hand to another in the time of need,
To be a cup of strength to a soul in a crisis of weakness
That is to know the glory of life.

THE END

Other books which may interest you

Available online from
www.spiritualtruthfoundation.org

Other books which may interest you

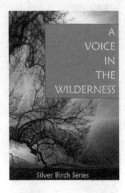

Available online from
www.spiritualtruthfoundation.org

Other books which may interest you

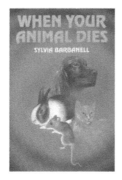
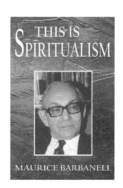

Available online from
www.spiritualtruthfoundation.org